Praise for *No More Blue Mondays*

"This is straight talk about what it takes to succeed and to love your work—every day of the week. Robin Sheerer and the four keys have helped me reenergize my career more than once."

Kathleen M. Flanagan, Vice President, Corporate Communications
The John Nuveen Company

"*No More Blue Mondays* is both empowering and practical. Filled with anecdotes, the book is the proverbial kick in the pants many people need. Robin Sheerer 'talks straight'—straight to the heart of the matter. Great for those seeking a powerful 'what's next?' for their career."

Aleen Bayard, Deputy Director, Public Relations
A.T. Kearney, Inc.

"Robin Sheerer has the unique ability to teach you how to see opportunities in your life, to find your passion, to live your dreams, and to make a difference personally and professionally."

Marc Adelman, Principal
The Environments Group

"In this very readable book, the author helps readers revitalize their work life with both uplifting 'internal' exercises and very practical action steps. The book speaks effectively to both the 'head and heart.' "

Richard Knowdell, Executive Director,
Career Planning and Adult Development Network,
Author of Building a Career Development Program

Anna,
Best wishes for great
Mondays!
Robie H. Sleeres

no more
blue
mondays

no more
blue
mondays

four keys to finding fulfillment at work

robin a. sheerer

Davies Black Publishing
Palo Alto, California

Published by Davies-Black Publishing, an imprint of Consulting Psychologists Press, Inc., 3803 East Bayshore Road, Palo Alto, CA 94303; 800-624-1765.

Special discounts on bulk quantities of Davies-Black books are available to corporations, professional associations, and other organizations. For details, contact the Director of Book Sales at Davies-Black Publishing, an imprint of Consulting Psychologists Press, Inc., 3803 East Bayshore Road, Palo Alto, CA 94303; 650-691-9123; Fax 650-623-9271.

Visit the Davies-Black Publishing web site at www.cpp-db.com

Cover photograph © Alan Sirulnikoff/Photonica

03 02 01 00 99   10 9 8 7 6 5 4 3 2
Printed in the United States of America

Library of Congress Cataloging-in-Publication Data
Sheerer, Robin A.
    No more blue mondays : four keys to finding fulfillment at work / Robin A. Sheerer.
       p. cm.
    Includes index.
    ISBN 0-89106-131-2
    1. Job satisfaction. 2. Career development. I. Title.
HF5549.5.J63S473   1999
650—dc21

                                                   98-31585
                                                       CIP

FIRST EDITION
First printing 1999

In memory of my mother,
Dorothy Sheerer,
an inspiring role model
and ultimately my best friend

contents

preface

I am convinced that work can be a great gift. Work provides a focus for our lives, grants us an identity, and is the single greatest arena available to us for self-expression, contribution, and personal growth.

"Who we are" is played out every day in the way we work. We are presented with the choice of being victims or being personally empowered. We can succumb to cynicism and despair in our work and our lives, or we can use whatever happens to us as an opportunity, responding in a number of positive ways:

- Expressing courage and faith
- Acting with integrity
- Being creative, innovative, and generative
- Expressing love, compassion, honesty, and humor
- Growing up

- Tapping into inspiration, intuition, empathy, and strength
- Being guided by our hearts

I hope you view work this way, too, and are reading this book for reinforcement. But perhaps, like the vast majority of people, you experience work as a burden and wish it could be more satisfying and enjoyable. It can be. I offer as proof the thousands of people I have known and worked with as a career coach since 1981 who are now fulfilled and empowered in their work and lives. This book is about how they made it happen and how you can, too.

This book is for you if you

- Don't know what you want to be when you grow up (regardless of your age)
- Are wondering whether you should stay with or leave your current job
- Are frustrated in your work and feel underutilized, bored, restless, or not challenged
- Know what you want to do but are scared to take the next steps
- Think there must be something more but don't want to leave your current job
- Feel depressed, in despair, or resigned about work
- Have been fired or laid off and fear that it happened because something is wrong with you
- Are not making any progress in a job search and are beginning to feel discouraged or panicked
- Are "burned out" or feel victimized, abused, or wronged in your job
- Plan to retire and want to create a new life that includes work of some kind

- Yearn for a life outside of work and don't know how to create it
- Feel insecure about your future with your company
- Want to have more influence or be a leader
- Think you no longer belong in your company because it has changed
- Have an idea for a business you want to start or would like to be self-employed
- Have accomplished your goals and don't know what to do next
- Don't even know what you want but just know that something is missing
- Want a dose of inspiration

If any of this describes you, dive in.

This book is divided into four parts. Part One introduces you to the four keys to finding fulfillment at work. Part Two guides you in creating an empowering work situation and a satisfying life where you are right now. Part Three is about leaving and how to do it well. Part Four focuses on staying on track in your work and life and offers help in figuring out what might be wrong if you find yourself unable to get moving. Every chapter concludes with questions to ask yourself, action steps to take, and reminders to apply the four keys.

You'll get great benefit from reading this book on your own, but it will be even more powerful (and fun) if you do it with other people. Gather together a small group of friends to create a seminar based on the book and establish just one rule: no griping without action. The support you provide for one another to "do" the book will lead to great results—I promise.

Over the last seventeen years, I've had the great privilege of working with people who were in the midst of changing their lives.

This book presents many of my clients' stories—examples of how they created exciting, challenging, and deeply satisfying work for themselves, some by staying with their jobs and some by leaving. I have disguised their names and circumstances for anonymity, but their stories are real. I hope I have captured their courage and strength. Their adventures have been a continuing source of inspiration to me, and I hope now they will be for you, too.

Robin A. Sheerer
February 1999

thank you

- To all of my clients who have entrusted me with their concerns, hearts, and dreams over the last seventeen years. I am humbly aware that when people are confronting a work-related crisis, it's a time of great vulnerability and intimacy. Thank you for the privilege of working with you at such an important juncture.

- To my writing support group: Les Lindeman, Paige Grant, Monica Paxson, Nancy Hill, and Gary McCabe. I couldn't have done it without you. Specifically, a big thank-you to Les, an established writer, for being one of the first to believe in me and gently pushing me along all these years; to Monica for your vast knowledge, wisdom, and powerful listening; to Paige for your enduring optimism and commitment to never letting anyone settle for less; to Nancy for your courage, humor, and poetry as well as a unique understanding of feminine gifts and power; to

Gary for jumping right in and using us like crazy to finish a book in no time and for your straightforward feedback.

- To Marsha Haake for working side by side with me for seven years at Career Enterprises. You are a gifted trainer and a deeply committed and insightful coach, and are leading the way as a spiritual guide.

- To the staff at Davies-Black Publishing, a great team to work with. Special thanks to Melinda Adams Merino, Acquisitions Editor, for nurturing me as a first-time author. I appreciate your enthusiastic support, respectful listening, and suggestions that greatly improved the book. And to Laura Simonds, Director of Sales, thanks for your tireless efforts to promote the book and teach me how to do it. And to Jill Anderson-Wilson, Managing Editor, for making it painless and easy.

- To Stephen Corrick, my agent at Mind Into Matter, for taking me on faith and believing in this book right from the beginning. Thanks for a level of commitment that extends far beyond the signing of the contract.

- To Marc Adelman, Flora Herron, Aleen Bayard, Jonathan Miller, John Balkcom, and Julie Baeb for generously contributing your time to make a promotional video.

- To Judy and Tim Maloney for generously opening your beautiful home in Sedona so I could spend time writing there. Being there with the two of you led to a breakthrough in my writing.

- To Sid Fey, Jack Chapman, Kathy Flanagan, Marti Beddoe, Kathy Erwin, Bobbye Middendorf, and Peter LeBrun for your feedback, constant encouragement, and support to write the book.

- To Rich Lessor, for being with me as a spiritual guide and mentor through several major transitions in my life, including the birth of this book.

- To all the people who selflessly assisted at workshops, and/or worked for Career Enterprises at some point in the last seventeen years, for your generosity and commitment to people and this work.

- To my patient mother-in-law, Viola Lemberger, and my stepsons, Brian and David, for putting up with my preoccupation with the book on many vacations and for your interest in its progress.

- To my beloved brother, Ben, for sharing my excitement and pride, and Judy, my sister-in-law, for your lifelong friendship and feedback on the book.

- To my husband, Earl Lemberger, who has lived with this book as long as I have. Thank you for sacrificing vacations, giving me the space to create, and always seeing me bigger than I see myself. I love you and treasure our partnership.

part one

the four keys to finding fulfillment at work

There's nothing else I would rather be doing.

—all the people I know who love their work

chapter 1
a path to great mondays

"Thank God it's Friday" keeps running through your head. You can't wait for the weekend. Friday is the best day of the week because of the anticipation. Saturday is good, too, but not great. Negative thoughts about work keep intruding, and you are aware of an underlying, low-level tension. Depression hits on Sunday. By evening, you're on the telephone talking to commiserating friends about how much you dread going to work tomorrow. They do, too.

Is this your life, or some variation of it? Do you even know any people who love their work and look forward to Mondays? I do—lots of them. If you're not one of them, you can be. There's hope. Helping people to create satisfying and fulfilling careers for themselves and become empowered in their work has been my focus for many years. I'm excited that I can share with you the successes my clients have had, how they did it, and how you can, too.

You'll be introduced to four keys to finding fulfillment at work that absolutely *work*. I have used them successfully in my own life, and so have thousands of other people in theirs. The four keys will work for you, too, whether you are new to the work world, have been employed for a while, or are considering retirement and a new work life. Take a moment to complete Assessment 1 to discover your current level of job satisfaction.

I come to my work as a career coach honestly. I have had serious bouts of blue Mondays in the past, and I experienced a major career crisis at the age of thirty-seven. Even though I had already changed careers twice, I still did not know what I wanted to be when I grew up or what I wanted to do next. I was also coming to terms with the fact that a master's degree is not a career plan.

Rather than looking for a quick fix in another job change, I decided to take the time to confront head-on the question of what I wanted to do with my life. That led to an exciting process of exploration that was both internal and external. As a result, I discovered a passion for the field of training and development—a kind of "coming home" experience for me—and a focus for my work that turned out to be a calling. I also acknowledged a fact that was true for me: I didn't want to work for anyone else ever again. Both discoveries were surprises to me.

Although I loved the discovery process, it wasn't easy. It was particularly hard to carry out alone. That's when I realized that many people could use help in figuring out what kind of work is a good fit for them. Four years later, I stepped away from a salaried teaching job, and since 1981 I have helped thousands of people find work they are passionate about and creative ways to handle a multitude of work-related issues. I've helped people change jobs, change careers, start or build businesses, and create change right where they were. I've worked one-on-one with people and led workshops and support groups. I've set up career development centers

assessment 1
is this you?

	True	False

*Check those statements that are true
for you right now.*

1. I constantly complain about work.   __   __

2. I spend too much money on treats
   (clothes, cars, vacations) to make
   up for the stress and disappointments at work.   __   __

3. I often daydream about different
   work and a different life.   __   __

4. My body is present at work, but my
   spirit and heart are not.   __   __

5. I find it hard to get up in the morning
   because I dread going to work.   __   __

6. I check the employment listings
   in the classified section every week.   __   __

7. I think a lot about making a change
   at work, but I haven't done anything
   because I keep hoping things will
   get better.   __   __

Add up the number of check marks in each column to find out where
you stand in regard to job satisfaction.

0 True: You're in great shape, but there's a whole new level of satisfaction, fulfillment, and self-expression for you to discover in your work.
Read on.

1–3 True: You're on the edge. Read on to discover how to avoid "blue
Mondays" and create work and a life you love.

4–7 True: It's definitely time for a change. Don't despair. Read on and
learn how to join the ranks of people who are empowered in their
work and love what they do.

within companies and coached employees. I've worked with people at all levels in almost every industry, from shop floor worker to CEO. With *all* of them, I have used the four keys as the foundation of our work together. Now you also have the opportunity to apply them to your life. Chart 1 introduces the four keys to finding fulfillment at work.

chart 1
the four keys to finding fulfillment at work

1. Reveal what's true for you.
2. Reclaim your personal power.
3. Express your commitment.
4. Surround yourself with support.

Key #1: Reveal what's true for you

What's true for you may not be true for anyone else you know. This truth is a personal truth. It's *your* bottom line. It's what's underneath your denial, stoicism, or confusion. When you say it out loud, it just feels right. If you share your discovery with others who know you well, they say, "Of course."

Simply saying the truth can be transforming. Remember how life-changing it was when you admitted any of the following truths?

- You would never feel whole until you completed your college education.

- You had to leave your family business if you were ever to grow up.

- You had outgrown your job and needed to move on.

- You were an artist and would never be happy unless you were creating things.
- You loved to start things but couldn't stand implementing them.
- You were so consumed and exhausted by your work that the only way you could decide what was next was to take a sabbatical.
- You no longer fit in your company (or industry) after it changed.
- You no longer found your work fun or exciting.

It takes courage to tell the truth, even to yourself, but doing so has the power to alter your life.

Reveal what's true for you

➡ Are you doing work that you really love? If not, what would that be?

➡ Are you fully contributing your talents, skills, and abilities, the qualities that make you unique, where you are right now?

➡ Do you have a personal vision, mission, or purpose in your work that inspires you?

➡ Are you taking risks, growing, or stretching in some way in your work?

➡ Do you support your boss? Are you fully on the team? If not, why are you there?

Revealing the truth lays the foundation for an empowered work situation and a satisfying life, but it is not enough. It has to be accompanied by action. That's key #2.

Key #2: Reclaim your personal power

You have lots of company if you feel stuck or think it's not your fault that you're unhappy at work. The simple truth, however, is that you have forgotten to reclaim your personal power through ownership and action.

Owning the situation you're in is not easy. It's always easier to blame other people or circumstances, but doing so leaves you feeling powerless. I have worked with many people who have been fired. Almost without exception, they start to take hold of their lives again when they admit that they should have left long ago but lacked the courage to do so. Their spirit had actually left long before they were fired. The question to ask yourself in order to own whatever is happening to you at any given time (including times of conflict with a boss or co-worker) is this: "If I were responsible for this situation right now, in what way would that be?" Taking ownership puts the *I* back into the equation. Maybe "they" can't or won't do anything about your situation, but you can. Even with an event you had nothing to do with, such as a layoff, you can reclaim your personal power by managing your reaction and what you do about it.

The second part of reclaiming your personal power involves taking action: doing something, almost anything, just not being, as one of my clients said, "like a deer caught in the headlights." Most of us spend a lot of time thinking and complaining about problems at work but doing very little about them. We wait and hope that things will get better. Getting into action relieves fear and depression. It is the energy behind an empowered work and life. And don't

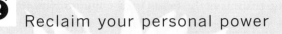

② Reclaim your personal power

- Are you taking action, such as making requests or volunteering for projects, instead of waiting to see what will happen?
- Are you acknowledging yourself for your accomplishments? Are you acknowledging everyone around you for theirs?
- Are you completing communications with people you have difficulty working with, or are you ignoring obvious tensions?
- Are you looking to see what's wanted and needed, what's missing (in your department, company, or industry), and acting on that?
- Are you continuing to grow and learn in your job, work, or business?

forget: saying what's true for you to someone who can make a difference may be your first action step to take.

Personal power is the energy in an empowered work situation and a satisfying life. Still, by itself it is not enough. The glue is missing. That's key #3.

Key #3: Express your commitment

With almost no company today providing guaranteed employment, it is empowering to understand the difference between being committed and being attached. Like most of us, you are probably attached to your work or job and your way of living. Yet everything changes; nothing lasts forever. You can work and live with commitment but not be attached to a particular job, industry, or lifestyle.

Here are some great ways to express your commitment:

- Make a choice (career direction, job, school, place to live, company to work for, whether to start a business).
- Put a stake in the ground (take the first step toward moving, starting a business, applying to schools).
- Get clear about what you stand for (quality, integrity, excellence, diversity, fairness, creativity).
- Decide where you want to put your energy.
- Do whatever it takes to get the job done.
- Give it everything you've got as long as it lasts.
- Manage yourself through the ups and downs.
- Coordinate your actions with your commitments.
- Hold on to your dream or vision.
- Stick with it.
- Be willing to start over.

③ Express your commitment

- ➡ Are you clear about what you are committed to (a particular career direction, goals, a way of working)?
- ➡ Are you coordinating your actions with your commitments rather than your feelings?
- ➡ Are you holding fast to your vision for your work and not giving in to cynicism or resignation?
- ➡ Do you keep on auditioning your great ideas and proposals, even in the face of repeated rejections?

Commitment is the glue in an empowered and fulfilling work situation and a satisfying life. But how do you keep going through thick and thin? That's where key #4 comes in.

Key #4: Surround yourself with support

Do you consider it a sign of weakness to ask for help or even to solicit different perspectives or ideas? Are you afraid you will be diminished in the eyes of other people if you let them see you can't do it all yourself? Are you trying to figure everything out by yourself or tough it out alone? Going it alone is guaranteed to create suffering. It is definitely a way to get into trouble at work, especially today when everything is so complex. We need each other's help in order to get our jobs done. We need support in remembering our visions, expanding our contributions, and accomplishing our dreams.

Like commitment, support can take multiple forms. Look to see how you are creating support in four different arenas in your life: emotional, intellectual, spiritual, and physical. For example, advice or help is just one form of emotional support; the right kind of confrontation can be another. You may remember a pivotal time in your life when someone was brutally honest with you. It was painful and you didn't like it, but it changed your life. That's support, too.

Cheerleading is a familiar form of emotional support. We all need people who believe in us and see us bigger than we see ourselves when we are feeling small. Books and tapes can provide both emotional and intellectual support. In the physical arena, our work and living environments can be designed to support our dreams and goals. Incorporating spiritual practices into our life can provide energy and a feeling of connection.

Surround yourself with support

➥ Have you left the "Ain't it awful?" club, the modern-day version of a Greek chorus, and joined a "Hallelujah chorus" of supportive people?

➥ Do you consciously choose to inspire yourself by reading positive books and articles and listening to motivating tapes?

➥ Have you surrounded yourself with people who are strong enough to talk "straight" to you?

➥ Do you ask for help when you need it? And have you learned to say no when you need to?

➥ Have you incorporated spiritual practices into your daily life?

Support is the spirit that infuses an empowered work situation and a satisfying life. The four keys to finding fulfillment at work—reveal what's true for you, reclaim your personal power, express your commitment, and surround yourself with support—are tools you can use again and again to empower your work and life. They can be applied throughout a lifetime of work and to a multitude of changes.

Open your heart and mind

Perhaps your first thought is that you will have to leave your current job in order to find work you love, feel satisfied and fulfilled, and be empowered. Maybe you will, and maybe you won't. I have discovered, to my surprise, that it's really hard for most people to leave their jobs even if they are unhappy. When I first started leading my career workshops, I thought I was failing because so many of the participants ended up staying in their jobs. When I talked to them later, though, I discovered that work had become very different for them since they had applied the four keys. They felt more committed, more productive, and more satisfied than ever before.

Why do so many people stay with jobs that they find unfulfilling? First, most of us are remarkably loyal unless we are working under terrible conditions, and sometimes we are even then. Most of us are also reluctant to step into an unknown situation. Besides that, it is not easy to create a new life while working full-time. It's possible, but not easy. Given all these factors, leaving is usually our last choice.

Yet after working with thousands of people, I have concluded that the key to making a good decision about whether to stay is to give yourself permission to consider leaving. Just open your heart and mind to new possibilities. If you don't give yourself the freedom to leave, you will always feel victimized by your job. But at the same time give yourself permission to explore options fully where you are right now. Then choose.

Opening your heart means learning to listen to your yearnings, even if they are just faint whispers: "I want to write a book." "If only I could be in charge. I want to run something myself." "I want to contribute more. I want to give more back to society." "I'm dying to spend more time with my kids." "I need to do something creative." These yearnings may not appear rational in your present circumstances, but that's not important at this stage of the game. What is important is that you open up to them and listen respectfully.

Opening your mind involves suspending judgment and exploring lots of possibilities. Like the vast majority of people, you probably "fell into" your job rather than actively choosing it. Exploring other possibilities will open your eyes and give you a new perspective on your current work. You may even discover that not only is the grass not greener on the other side, but also it is only grass. If you explore fully first, then whatever you decide will be a true choice, and if your decision is to stay where you are, it will be a totally different experience. Opening your mind means looking at the whole picture before getting into the details.

Empower your dreams, not your complaints

Are you ready to be inspired? Here is how one person took herself from an unhappy work situation to a happy one, using the four keys as her guide. Notice that at the beginning of the process, even though Martha was self-employed, she still felt disempowered and victimized. It's easy to do.

A dream come true

Martha was forty years old and self-employed as an editor when we met. Her business was limping along, and she was struggling. She felt isolated, lonely, and underpaid. Martha attended my workshop and a support group afterward. She then went on to create a new life for herself. I had not heard from her in many years when I received a letter from her.

She reminded me that after the workshop she had been inspired to get her master's degree in computer science. She then worked for a company for several years, but in the back of her mind she always dreamed about leaving the city, moving to a rural area, and getting into business for herself again. Then a friend moved to a small town in Kentucky to work for a large company and brought Martha in as a consultant. She fell in love with the community. "It is a small . . . rural farming community, with charming buildings, built in a hilly area," she wrote in her letter. "Two restaurants, one grocery store, five churches, one hardware store, and a thriving artist colony (pottery, carvers, weavers, etc.)."

Martha bought an old home on two acres, with the idea of moving in about three years later. Then, unexpectedly, a company representative asked Martha whether she'd be interested in a six-month on-site assignment. She said yes and moved into the house she had bought. The consulting assignment was extended, and Martha settled into the town. The next spring, she fulfilled another dream by opening a quilt shop, selling supplies for quilters (fabric, patterns, books, muslin, quilt gift items, etc.) and teaching quilting classes. She was now working with her hands as well as her head, something she had always wanted to do. She reported that she had never been happier in her life: "Peaceful living environment, birds, squirrels, rabbits, coons, etc., in the backyard. Peaceful working environment. . . . And I met a wonderful local guy. . . . We are engaged and will be married."

As Martha concluded, "Taking more and more steps in the direction of our dreams is addictive." ●

Many of my clients have used the four keys to create fulfilling work and satisfying lives for themselves, some right where they were and others after they left their jobs. Read about the four keys in the following chapters to learn how you can, too.

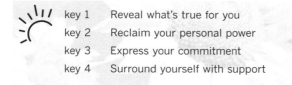

key 1   Reveal what's true for you
key 2   Reclaim your personal power
key 3   Express your commitment
key 4   Surround yourself with support

Questions to ask yourself

- What do I have a yearning to do?

- How would I complete this sentence? If only I could _____.

- What work or life change would improve my health, give me peace of mind, and increase my happiness?

Action steps to take

- Form a support group with people who are as committed to change as you are. Use this book as a focus for your discussions, and use the action steps as homework. Meet every two to three weeks to keep the momentum going.

- Interview someone who is living his or her life the way you want to live yours. Ask that person how he or she did it.

- Tell three people you trust what you sometimes dream you would like to do, and ask them how *they* would make it happen. (Do not ask them for advice about how *you* should do it.)

- Write a description of your ideal life—what would it look like? Where would you be? What work would you be doing?

By telling myself the truth, I was able to allow myself to do what I wanted to do.

—a happy career changer

chapter 2
key #1: reveal what's true for you

Remember that what's true for you should be the foundation for your life and your work. A great place to start is with how you feel about the job you have right now. Use this scale to begin telling the truth.

On a scale of 1 to 10, how do you feel about your current work?

1	3	5	7	10
I hate it	It's a living	It's okay	It's good	I'm passionate about it

What would it take to make it a 10? What's missing for you? Even if you're at 7 and have a job most people would die for, work for a respected company with great people, or earn lots of money, you may not be excited about going to work. It's okay to want something more.

There's nothing better than loving your work. Have you ever noticed that people who love what they do exude energy and their eyes sparkle? Best of all, they don't complain about work constantly. They even look forward to Mondays. They're a joy to be around, and their enthusiasm is contagious.

On the other hand, there is nothing worse than dreading work. It is such a big part of life that being unhappy at work casts a dark cloud over everything. Environments can become toxic, and people can, too.

I'm convinced that only a few people seem to know almost from the moment they are born what work they want to do. Most people "fall into" their work, and only a small number end up loving it. For the rest of us, discovering the right fit takes effort and time. It's definitely a process, not an event, but it's well worth it.

The most powerful action you can take to create fulfilling work and a life you love is to tell the truth about what really lights you up and then build your life around that. By putting your passions first, not last, you will add fire to your life and gain the will to figure out how to make it all work.

What are you passionate about?

The first step in uncovering your passions is to become an astute observer of yourself. Observing is not analyzing. It requires the ability to stand back and look without judging. For many reasons, most of us are unpracticed at this. We conduct our lives at high speed and don't stop long enough to reflect. We consider reflection a luxury we can't afford. But making wise choices requires slowing down to see and hear what's on the inside as well as the outside. It's not a luxury when your life energy is on the line. The decisions you make will determine the direction and quality of your life for many years to come.

You will get into serious trouble in your work and life if you follow advice from co-workers, bosses, and family more willingly than you follow advice from your own heart. For instance, when you are conducting a job search, people may advise you to "look in the industries where the jobs are plentiful." However, this disregards the question of whether the work is a good fit for you. People who give such advice are usually talking from their own fears or preferences rather than from an understanding of what would be a life-affirming choice for you. They are the same people who will caution you to be "realistic" or "practical," advice that is one-dimensional. As a human being you are not one-dimensional. You are capable of listening to your heart, defining your own reality, and being practical, too.

Sometimes passions are deeply buried, and sometimes they are so obvious that you dismiss them. Learn to look for clues to your passions in everyday life. Once I received a big clue by noticing what I was currently reading. Although I was a practicing psychotherapist and teacher at the time, I noticed that I was not reading material related to either of those professions. Instead, I was devouring books about personal growth training. I was also beginning to design training workshops in my head. The clues to my passions were all around me; I just hadn't seen them.

Start with the areas you would say are closest to your heart: passions, yearnings, and the interests you love most. Figuring out how to turn these into paid work comes later. First, give yourself permission to explore any and all passions, no matter how absurd, outrageous, or unrealistic they may initially appear in terms of work possibilities.

The following questions will help you uncover your passions. Focus on the *you* in each question. This is not about what other people want for you, and it's not about what you think you *should* want. It's about what's true for you. So for now, look into your work and every other area of your life, suspend any related concerns and fears, and *tell the truth,* answering the questions honestly and from your heart.

What gives you energy or "juice" when you're doing it, rather than leaving you feeling depleted?   You can keep at such an activity for hours. After a long time, you may experience some normal fatigue, but with a short rest you can get going again. What are you doing when it's like this for you?

What totally absorbs you?   What are you doing when the hours fly by and you don't even notice that it has gotten dark or you forgot to eat? What are you doing when *you* are lost and there is nothing present but what you are doing (no grocery or "to do" lists, no awareness of aches and pains, no thoughts about football or basketball or even sex)? What are you doing when you are "in the flow"?

What do you daydream about?   Pay attention to thoughts such as these: "If I ran a bed-and-breakfast, I'd do it this way." "I'd think I was in heaven if I did this all day long." "Boy, it would be neat to help fix lots of small businesses." "I'd love to live in the mountains, write books, and consult with companies four to six days a month."

What do you have strong opinions about and talk about to everyone who will listen?   Is there a theme to these opinions? For example, what would you love to champion, create policy or campaign for, or represent?

What do you think you can do better than anyone else?   What do you care about more than other people seem to? Where do you want to lead the way?

What do you head for in the bookstore?   What do you never get tired of reading? Look around, and pay attention to what you are reading these days. (For one of my clients, the answer to this question was "The whole bookstore." That was her clue that she should be a librarian, and she went back to school to get a master's degree in library science.)

When asked "What can't you get enough of?" what answer would you give?   What do you never tire of doing or of reading, talking, or thinking about?

What interest or activity would you say is "in your blood"?   There maybe a particular activity that you grew up around or have been doing or hearing about since childhood. It's just natural to you. Maybe you never took it seriously before now. One client told me that when he went for walks in his neighborhood, he always stopped in front of buildings and imagined how he would arrange the furniture and decorate the apartments inside—didn't everyone?

What interest or hobby consumes you?   What do you find yourself spending hours and hours with in your "spare" time?

What are you talking about when you "light up like a Christmas tree"? What subject makes you "come to life"? When you talk about it, your eyes sparkle, you smile a lot, and you become very animated, gesturing or moving your whole body as you talk.

What has been a recurring theme in your life, showing up repeatedly in one form or another throughout the years, starting as early as childhood?   Clues about our passions are often embedded in our childhood. They show up very early. For example, were you one of those kids who made up plays, put your pals into roles, helped build the set, sold tickets, and then served as master of ceremonies? I met a little girl like this recently. I was camping on a Fourth of July weekend, sitting in front of the trailer reading, when I heard a little voice saying, "Oh, Miss, Miss!" I turned around and saw three little girls, ranging in age from three to eight. The eight-year-old said, "We'd like to do a play for you." She then proceeded to lead the other two in waving little flags, singing patriotic songs, riding bikes, and marching around in a circle. Earlier, I had heard her organizing the other two and ordering them to rehearse.

If you could do anything you wanted to do, what would it be?   Assume that you don't have to worry about money, age, background, or anything; just let your mind go!

Answering these questions takes some time. Again, it's a process, not an event. Often, it takes three months to a year, and sometimes even longer. First of all, it takes reflective work, and that can be done in one of several ways: doing exercises from career books; writing in a journal; taking long, solitary walks; or meeting regularly to talk about the questions with a career coach or a couple of friends. Usually, the answers don't come to you if you do nothing, and they seldom hit like a bolt of lightning. It's more as if they sneak up on you. You begin to notice that some answers keep showing up again and again. Your job is to take them seriously, even those that seem ridiculous or unlikely. This book is full of true stories about people who have successfully created work lives and lifestyles they love, some of which were initially considered very unrealistic, even by me (and I am the eternal optimist about people doing the work they love). Bruce's story is one of them.

Trains

Bruce was thirty-three and miserable in his job in banking when he attended my career workshop. He was also married and the father of two young children. His wife was not working outside the home, so his income was necessary for the family. When Bruce explored where the passion in life was for him, the answer kept coming up "trains."

Bruce had adored trains since childhood. He collected trains, made models, played with them, and read constantly about them. But a career dealing with them seemed like an impossible dream. What could he do now, at his age? Nevertheless, I encouraged Bruce to consider a career change. On the first evening of the two-day workshop, he began talking to his wife about it. He anticipated that she would be angry and upset with him. Instead, she slipped a note in his jacket pocket that said "Keep the vision"; he found it the next day. After the workshop, Bruce's wife called to thank me for giving her back the enthusiastic man she had married ten years before.

Bruce got to work pursuing his dream. He did everything he needed to make a career change and was willing to start at the bottom in his chosen field as a conductor, believing he would move up quickly. Today, he works as a manager for a major railroad. Because of his previous work experience and his passionate commitment to the industry, he was able to move up quickly.

After his first day of work, Bruce wrote me a letter saying it was the first time as a working adult he had felt at home. He was finally with people who were as crazy about trains as he was. ●

Finding work you love is often an experience of "coming home." It feels right. It's comfortable. Everything you did before now makes sense and looks as if it was leading up to this. The people around you seem like true colleagues in spirit. There is a harmony to it all. Your life takes on new meaning, and you are filled with energy.

Sometimes your passions are like hot coals, firing your imagination, energizing you, and filling your thoughts or activities. And sometimes they are only warm coals because you indulge them infrequently. In either case, you need to fan them into flames if they are to become the focus of your work and life. Do it by immersing yourself in what you love, even if you are already working full-time.

- Spend time with people who are currently doing what you think you want to do.

- Join a group dedicated to your interest. If you can't find one, form one yourself. I have several clients who have done this very successfully. One person formed a group of computer consultants, who talk about solving computer problems. Another formed a group of artists, who meet monthly to share ideas and stimulate creativity. Recently, they even took a trip together to an artists' colony.

- Take classes. I am amazed at how many adults resist attending classes after they have graduated from school, whether they have a high school education or a Ph.D. degree. Artists and writers are some of the worst offenders. Regardless of your age or skill level, it is arrogant to assume you have nothing more to learn. Take a class, for three reasons: (1) you will probably learn something, even if you are highly skilled and experienced; (2) you will benefit from being exposed to a structure that enhances productivity (it's called "homework"); and

(3) you will be inspired by associating with colleagues who are as passionate about the subject area as you are.

- Read everything about your area of interest that you can get your hands on.

- Attend events related to your passion and join and participate in a professional association related to it.

- Volunteer your services or create an internship to spend time doing and learning what you love.

Give yourself to the things that interest you. Surround yourself with them. It may take time, but doing so will give you energy, not deplete you. As a result of this immersion, a path may open up for you to make a living at what you love.

Perhaps the major reason you do not pursue what really interests you is fear about money. You may have a hard time imagining that you could do work you really love *and* make enough money to support yourself. Most people have a predictable, knee-jerk response of "But I can't afford to do it" whenever they start thinking about what they would really love to do. However, my years as a career coach have convinced me that this is a problem people handle when they become clear about what they really want and make a commitment to it. They find amazingly creative and resourceful ways to pursue their desires. In fact, almost all my clients have done as well financially—usually better—when they followed their hearts instead of their "shoulds."

Of course, not every passionate interest can lead directly or immediately to a living. We know that many artists, for instance, have a hard time financially. However, even among artists there are those who do very well financially, those who make just enough money to support their art, those who care more about their art than about money, and those who find other, deeply satisfying work that is closely related to the work they most love to do. On the basis of what I have seen, I can tell you that when you are committed, you will find a way to do what you want *and* make money. At that point, your passions become more important than your possessions, and simplifying your life doesn't feel like a sacrifice; it feels like a step in the right direction. Don't forget, too, that you may decide that some passions should remain hobbies. Perhaps you would not enjoy them as much if they were your full-time work; doing them on weekends or in the evenings is enough to enrich your life. At a minimum, choose work that interests you. Interests can be fueled and may turn into flames someday.

Often, our passions are hidden by a heavy cover of concerns: "I'm too old." "I'm too young." "I don't know the right people." "I don't have the right connections." "I don't have the money." "I don't know how to do it." "I'll never earn a living at it." If you get caught up in such concerns, you may never explore the possibilities fully. And if you do start to pursue them more seriously, you may be confronted by negative comments such as "You'll never make any real money doing that." "You're going to do *what*?" or "At *your* age?" If you take such comments too seriously, you may neglect to explore areas of interest on the basis of the reactions of a few friends who are unhappy and cynical about their own work choices. Or you may get bogged down in questions about how you could possibly make a change before you have even conducted a thorough search to discover where your heart is.

It's important to get all your fears about pursuing your passions out on the table. Ask yourself what you are afraid of. Is this something that might really happen, something you made up, or something you heard from other people? What's the worst thing that could happen to you if you pursue your passion? After examining your fears, fan your desire; don't fuel your fear! Make your choices from love, not fear.

You may be sacrificing your authenticity by trying to fit into some job you think you "should" be doing or "have to" continue doing because you have invested so many years in it, but it is never too late to examine your passions. You may even end up incorporating more of what you love to do right where you are. Being honest with yourself about your heart's desires is the first step in taking charge of your work and life and creating an exciting and fulfilling future. The next step often involves telling someone else who can make a difference, as Sarah did.

Sarah's request

When I first met Sarah, she was a lawyer who worked as legal counsel for a pharmaceutical company. She loved the company she worked for and enjoyed her co-workers. She was well paid and highly regarded, but she was thinking about leaving her job because she was bored and dissatisfied with legal work. She told me she wanted to be doing something more directly people oriented and more interesting to her.

When I asked Sarah whether she had talked to her manager about this, she said she hadn't because she feared he would consider her a poor team member if she complained. When she had evaluations with him, instead of revealing her true feelings she was generally upbeat and discussed only the work she was currently doing.

I gave Sarah some homework to help her clarify what she did want, and we worked on making a distinction between being a team player and asking for what she wanted in the spirit of making a bigger contribution at work. Then she got her courage up to talk to her manager. When she finally opened up to him, he was not only understanding but also responsive. As soon as an opening came up in the marketing department, he recommended Sarah for the position. She was thrilled about the new opportunity and the possibilities that were now available to her. Because Sarah always worked hard and did her job extremely well, her boss would never have known how unhappy she was if she had not told him. ●

What gives meaning to your work?

Do you find work meaningless and unfulfilling? This is one of the most common complaints I hear in my work as a career coach. Perhaps, like many of my clients, you find yourself in a high-paying job that has few rewards other than money but you feel trapped because of your current lifestyle.

Money can be one of the biggest obstacles to discovering work that is meaningful to you. When you are making a lot of money but are in the wrong job, you have to convince yourself that you are happy or reward yourself constantly with material gifts, rationalizing that you deserve them because you work so hard and are miserable. The trap gets deeper with each new purchase. The problem is that money is never really a motivator unless you need it for survival. After basic needs are met, money loses its motivating power almost immediately.

Just think about it. When you got your most recent raise, within a month your standard of living probably rose to meet it. Now it is lost in the budget. Even people who are in the money game, such as traders and investment managers, are not always happy in their work or motivated by money over the long term. Money cannot make up for everything else that's missing. Over the last twenty years, public opinion surveys and sociological research have shown repeatedly that people rate "the work itself" as a much more important motivator than money. So if you do not love your work or do not see it as serving a larger purpose, chances are it will become empty for you after a while.

Many people in business are artists in disguise and wonder why they are unhappy. After years of coaching people, I am convinced that being creative is not an option for artistic people; it's a *need*. Business is an industry that essentially requires the use of left-brain functions (thinking logically, linearly, and sequentially) and includes many jobs that do not lend themselves naturally to creativity. So if you are someone who usually leads with your right brain (seeing the big picture, being artistic, focusing on relationships), you may feel trapped, unhappy, and unappreciated in the business world.

Sometimes, taking on artistic projects outside of work can take care of the lack you are experiencing in your life. For instance, my friend Dave found a great way to be creative while keeping his technical writing business. After the initial excitement of starting a business wore off, Dave was bored, and his need for more creative expression increased. His business limped along, reflecting his personal state. He was close to closing it down when he began getting up early in the morning to do some creative writing. Then he added drawing and painting. He began to feel revitalized, and his business suddenly expanded and grew. As he explained, his artwork inspired everything else. He expanded his business by entering into a joint venture and building a computer-testing lab for customers. When he built the lab, he added a studio for himself, where he now escapes to play with his art every day. When Dave realized that he'd been waiting until he was rich to express his artistic side, he decided that maybe it's the other way around. He says now that if he never becomes rich, it doesn't matter because he is enjoying his life and his work more than ever before.

If you believe that you cannot leave your job and if you don't have the option of building an art studio where you work, as Dave did, the best thing you can do is figure out how to incorporate your passion for creativity into your life. Take art or cooking classes; join a band or chorus; write poems or novels; go dancing. Just feed the creative part of you. And remember that being creative doesn't necessarily mean being an artist. It can also mean being inventive, resourceful, or imaginative. Even if you don't consider yourself an artist, don't stop looking for ways to be creative in your work.

Perhaps being creative in your work is enough to allow you to feel that you are making a difference. But it may not be. You may need a purpose, or "calling," for your work. I agree that some work does not easily lend itself to a sense of purpose. You might find it hard to be inspired by selling certain products or doing certain kinds of work. However, if you cannot find a purpose *in* your work or *for* your work, you can look for it in *how* you do your work. Every encounter with another human being is an opportunity to touch someone's life. Think of the people around you who have jobs that might be considered menial but who elevate the jobs just by the way they do them. For example, my mother spent some time in a nursing home before she died. Nursing homes can be very grim places. The people who work there as nurse's aides are usually not highly paid and do very strenuous and difficult, even dangerous, work. Again and again, I was deeply moved by the cheerfulness and loving care that many of the aides at my mother's nursing home brought to their jobs. I will never forget a woman who picked up my mother from her chair and gently gave her a kiss as she laid her back down on her bed. Even if you have an ordinary job, you can be extraordinary in the way you do your work.

A sense of purpose provides continuity in your life. It is like a well of inspiration. It keeps you going in the darkest times (and there will be some, no matter how much you love what you do). It provides a focus to return to when you feel pulled in a thousand different directions. It helps you make work choices. When you clarify a purpose for yourself and look back on your past work experiences, suddenly they all make sense no matter how unrelated they seemed at the time. They now appear to have been natural steps, always leading you along the path.

How do you find your purpose in life? Often, it is a thread that has been woven throughout your life from the time you were very little. Some people articulate it as something external, such as "a world without hunger," "providing beauty to the world," or "being a bridge between cultures." Others describe it as something internal, saying "I try to be a conduit for good wherever I go" or "I want to bring peace and a sense of organization to every situation I find myself in." Usually, there is no single job or way to express your purpose; many choices can fit. The seeds of your true purpose may be in what you are doing right now, even though this may be hard to see. Your current frustration or disappointments may blind you to it. It may take a while to discover your purpose in life.

It's particularly important to sort out your feelings about your work when you have experienced a failure, burnout, or disappointment. When you are hurt, you may want to turn your back entirely on the past and to get as far away from it as possible. But it may have been only the circumstances that were wrong, not the work itself. In such a case, you need only find a job where the fit is right in order to blossom.

Sometimes people find their true purpose as a result of disturbing, even traumatic, circumstances such as a layoff, as Patricia did.

A layoff leads to purpose

Patricia attended my career workshop because she had lost her job as a supervisor in an information systems department as a result of a massive layoff and didn't have any idea what to do next. During the workshop, she realized that she wanted to create a business that provided energy breaks for people as an alternative to coffee breaks. She decided that one of her purposes in life was to support people's health and well-being. This focus was a natural one for Patricia. She had always loved body movement and had been a dancer for years. She decided to focus on providing massages as energy breaks and got herself trained in bodywork. She started her own business, giving fifteen-minute, fully clothed neck and back massages in the workplace and full-body massages in the privacy of her home.

Patricia turned out to be an excellent businesswoman, as well as an enthusiastic and generous teacher. Her business grew rapidly and seemingly with little effort on her part. She hired employees, took classes to increase her skills, and quickly became an acknowledged expert in the city where she lives. Her success has been so great that she has also been able to pursue a Ph.D. degree in a subject that interests her and travel extensively to other countries.   ●

Finding your purpose does not necessarily mean making a career change, as it did for Patricia; you may be able to fulfill your sense of purpose within your present career. To discover your purpose, look back at your whole life up to this point. Why do you think you are here? What are you meant to do? As a child, what did you think you would be doing when you were older to "fix" things in the world? What situations stir you up and make you angry?

What quality do you bring to every situation? Think about instances in which you felt impassioned and then took action. Ask yourself, "In each case, what seemed to be my purpose?" Then try saying, in the fewest words possible, "My purpose is _____." Keep working at it until it feels right for you. You can have more than one purpose, by the way. If it isn't clear to you right away, don't agonize over it. Let it be a question that floats in your consciousness as you go about your life, and an answer may begin to appear.

What would it look like to be authentically self-expressed?

Are you one of the huge number of people like my client Craig, who says, "I have to leave myself at the door when I go to work"? If so, you may be in the wrong job. I am convinced that work is the single greatest arena available to us for self-expression, but it's hard to believe this as you look at the faces of most people on their way to work or at their job.

Sometimes we do not see the opportunities available right where we are for expressing ourselves more fully. Or we consciously hold back because of past hurts and rejections. Or we are blind to the gifts we have to offer. When people first call me for help, it's usually because they are in pain about their work and feeling one of several ways: exhausted and "on empty"; resentful because they feel unappreciated for their efforts and abilities; taken advantage of, maybe even abused; stuck or plateaued; frustrated in their attempts to contribute; or confused about what's next. Regardless of the reason, their self-esteem is always low, even if they are viewed by others as very successful and talented. At this stage, they typically are out of touch with their gifts and believe they have nothing of value to offer. My job then is to help people recognize and appreciate their unique gifts, and contribute them fully.

You may be blind to your gifts because something you do exceptionally well is effortless for you. You tend to dismiss it as unimportant or as something everyone else does well, too. It's the "Doesn't everyone?" attitude. Your personal qualities (such as patience, curiosity, humor, and empathy) are just as important as your talents and skills (such as analyzing, organizing, convincing, and selling). Even your love for something is a great gift. Because these are such natural parts of you, perhaps you are overlooking them as clues to the work you could excel in and find immensely gratifying.

Women, I've found, often have a harder time than men identifying their gifts and talking about them. Their mothers have trained them to be modest and unassuming and not to not talk about themselves in a way that anyone could interpret as bragging. And many of the special qualities women have to contribute, such as sensitivity to relationships, historically have not been valued in the workplace, especially in the business world. They can hardly expect themselves to value something not valued by others, at least initially. It is no surprise to me that capable women are leaving companies in droves and starting their own businesses. I am convinced that this is due not only to lack of personal opportunities but also to work environments that don't value women's gifts and therefore inhibit their growth and development. Creative men whose talents have been overlooked and undervalued in the workplace (and there are plenty of them) also suffer.

However, it is a self-defeating exercise to blame everyone around you for the fact that you have not blossomed. Perhaps you work with the hope that someday, someone will notice how good you are and then develop and reward you. It is very seductive to think the world works this way, but there is ample evidence that it does not. You need to be responsible for recognizing your own gifts and finding a way or a place to express them fully.

Most of my clients initially have difficulty allowing themselves to be more expressive at work. They feel repressed, "shut down," and think that their environment is the cause. They usually make up rules in their heads about how they should dress and act and then never really question or challenge these rules. They look around and decide that they have to dress like everyone else, even if there isn't a dress code. They even decide that they will be fired if they do anything differently from everyone else. In business settings especially, many people decide that any part of themselves that is creative, fun, witty, or mischievous cannot be expressed, even though most businesses are begging employees to be more creative.

Suppressing yourself will erode your spirit and lead you to misrepresent yourself to the world at large. You may be thinking that you can't be yourself in your business environment. Maybe this is true; maybe not. Tom felt constrained by a business environment, too, but he found that being himself led to new success.

Tom loosens up

When Tom first met with Marsha, a consultant who worked for me, she thought he was a very uptight person, judging from the way he was dressed. His clothes were extremely conservative and bland business attire. Tom worked as an account executive for an advertising agency. He complained to Marsha about how unhappy he was in his work and what boring clients he had. He thought maybe he should leave the agency, even advertising as a whole, and do something else.

When Marsha asked Tom about things he liked to do outside of work, things that were exciting to him, he reported that he and his wife loved to explore "funky" little places—stores, restaurants, nightclubs. Marsha laughed and commented that she would never know it by looking at him. Tom went on to say that his only assignments at work were boring, stodgy accounts. Marsha pointed out that *he* looked boring and stodgy and asked him why he wasn't expressing this funky side of himself more at work. She suggested that he match his outside with his inside and start expressing that other part of himself in his present job.

Tom began by getting rid of his conservative ties and wearing some really wild ones that he loved. The response to them was positive. He began to loosen up and express himself more, giving voice to his offbeat sense of humor and different perspective on things. It was no surprise to Marsha when soon he was rewarded with a plum assignment—a major motorcycle account. It was a great match. Tom started loving his work and decided not to leave his company. ●

Tom had to make the first move. He had to express who he really was *before* landing work he loved, not land it and *then* express himself. It often takes courage to express who we really are, but you can see how easily we make up rules that constrain us. Advertising as an industry is much looser than most, but even so, Tom did not feel free to express himself.

You may worry that people will not like the "real" you, but you pay a high price if you act in a way that is not authentic or congruent with who you really are. By holding back, you not only deprive others of your gifts but you also end up lacking intimacy with yourself and others. You will be far more successful if you are natural and authentic, wherever you are. And if who you are is not tolerated, then it's best to leave and find the right "garden" to blossom in.

How do you recognize your own gifts? There are lots of career books with excellent exercises to help you do this. One of the best, in my eyes, is Richard Bolles's small book *The New Quick Job-Hunting Map* (Ten Speed Press, 1990). But please note it is a book to *do,* not read. It's well worth the effort. Another method is to ask your friends, family members, co-workers, and boss what they think your gifts are. When they answer, your job is to take a deep breath, say "Thank you," and let it in.

Even anger can be a clue to your gifts. When people become very angry about the way something is done or not done, it often is because they have a gift for seeing what's missing and are far ahead of everyone else. If you are someone who sees how something *should* be or recognizes injustice, sloppiness, lack of integrity, or mediocrity, perhaps it is because you have the gift of seeing those things clearly. Being furious with everyone for not seeing them is not responsible. Just acknowledge to yourself, with gratitude, that you are way out in front, and then go to work enrolling others in what you see as possible.

Too many people give up too easily on their companies as places where they can grow. Most of us suggest a new idea or make a request once or twice and then, if we are told no, decide it will never happen. Everyone should have some sales training to learn how to get through all the no's and reach a yes.

With all the restructuring and redesigning of companies going on today, there are plenty of chances to express yourself and contribute more at work. New opportunities are constantly opening up. You just need to be observant and look to see what's wanted and needed, what's missing, especially in areas where your talents fit. Then go after these opportunities. Don't wait to be invited.

Co-workers may not know what you are capable of. For example, they may not be aware of the fact that outside of work, you are a tiger. You write a wildly popular newsletter for your church, run extremely successful fund-raising campaigns for a nonprofit organization, or gracefully lead volunteer groups through difficult decision-making processes. How can they know this if you are timid at work, never volunteering for projects you're not sure you can manage well and hardly ever speaking up in staff meetings? You need to let people at work know what you *can* do and *want to* do, even if you have been disappointed in the past. Find a way to express your talents.

If you have given a 100 percent all-out effort to contribute more of who you are at your workplace and it is absolutely clear that there is no possible way for you to do it, there are two things you can do: (1) express yourself fully outside of work if you are not ready to leave your job; (2) put a plan in place to leave, and begin taking action.

Talents, skills, abilities, and special qualities are all gifts given to you by your Creator, and they are gifts you can give to others. Perhaps the only thing you owe your Creator is to use these gifts fully, to blossom during your lifetime.

	key 1	Reveal what's true for you
	key 2	Reclaim your personal power
	key 3	Express your commitment
	key 4	Surround yourself with support

Questions to ask yourself

- If I won the lottery, what would I do?
- If I took my "hobby" seriously, how could I make money at it? How could I expand it?

- What would I like to do more of?

- What do I want to give my life energy to? What would truly engage me?

- What has been a source of pain in my life? Is this an area in which I can discover my life's purpose?

- The next time you accomplish something that feels great, in any area of your life, ask yourself this: What seemed to be an underlying purpose or mission in the way I handled this?

- What do I need to accomplish before I die? What is the legacy I want to leave?

- What does everyone say I am really good at?

- What do people ask me to do because no one else does it as well?

- What talents, skills, abilities, or qualities show up again and again in my accomplishments?

Action steps to take

- Purchase career books and *do* the exercises in them; don't just read the books. Barbara Sher's book *I Could Do Anything If I Only Knew What It Was* (Delacorte Press, 1994), Nancy Anderson's *Work with Passion* (New World Library, 1995), and Richard Bolles's *The New Quick Job-Hunting Map,* mentioned earlier in this chapter, are three of the best you'll find. They're full of great exercises to help you uncover your passions.

- Work with a career coach who is committed to helping you find work that you love, not just another job.

- Find three people to interview who are openly passionate about their work. Ask them what they like most about it, what they like least about it, what a typical day or week is like for them, and whether they would make the same career choice if they could do it all over again.

- Interview a few people who seem to have a sense of mission in their work. Don't have all of them be in the nonprofit or health care fields; make sure at least one of them works in business. Ask them how they arrived at their sense of purpose.

- Wear something different to work that expresses who you are. Do this several times, and observe the reactions of people around you. If some people tease you about it, ask yourself whether there is envy underneath the teasing.

- Volunteer for something you know you are good at but have never done in your work setting before.

- Express your ideas everywhere you go, especially in settings where you usually do not talk. Do this even if someone else has already said the same thing.

One day, I looked at the outfit I had on and asked myself, "Who dressed you today?"

—a friend, in a conversation about
  taking responsibility

chapter 3
key #2: reclaim your personal power

Perhaps, like most people, you are in a trance when you are at work. You have forgotten that *you* are in charge of your life. You feel powerless to change things or influence events. Everything is "they" or "them." To shake yourself from your trance and regain your personal power, you must (1) take ownership of the circumstances you are in, no matter how difficult they are, and (2) get into action.

Ownership gives you power

Taking ownership of a difficult situation involves answering this question: If I *were* responsible in some way for this, how might that be? Your answers could surprise you. Rarely have I worked with someone who has been fired who didn't know that he or she should have left long before it reached that point. Many times, we see warning signs of trouble ahead even in our first interview for a job, but we ignore them because we're insecure or overly anxious to get work.

It's true that bad things happen to people at work, really unfair things that they have nothing to do with. But even in such cases, if you take ownership of the circumstances, the result can be personal growth and a better outcome than you ever imagined, as it was for Rob.

Colorado, here I come!

Rob was set up to fail in his job. After many years of good work as an auditor, he was transferred to a sales position as a result of a reorganization. The assignment didn't make sense, but Rob was willing to give it his best shot and learn how to sell. He was naturally gregarious and had great people skills, so he had a good chance of succeeding in the new job. The problem was that his new boss withheld advice and support. Rob's response to the situation was to take it as a challenge. In his first year, he sold more than anyone else on the team.

His boss then upped the ante, setting impossible goals and putting obstacles in the way to prevent Rob from achieving them. By this time, Rob was pretty well convinced that his boss was out to get rid of him because Rob was homosexual, but there was nothing he could prove. Rob came to me in disgust and despair.

After thinking through the situation carefully, Rob decided it was not worthwhile for him to sue the company. He took ownership of the situation, acknowledging that he didn't want to stay in the present work environment and was ready to move on anyway. He decided that the bad treatment was a gift. It gave him the impetus to leave.

Rob got into action. He kept his head high at work, continued to be productive, and began exploring ideas to find out what he wanted to do. He finally made the commitment to return to auditing and look for work in Colorado, where he had dreamed of living for many years. Almost immediately, he was offered a job as an account manager, a perfect fit for him. It included a huge raise. Within a week, Rob put his house on the market, sold it, and found a new place to live. Two days after he left the company, he flew to Colorado to start a new life.

Two months later, I got a letter from Rob expressing how happy he was in Colorado and how appreciated and comfortable he felt in his new job. He also told me he had met a potential mate. He concluded that the job change was the best thing that ever could have happened to him. ●

Just get into action: do something, anything

Are you waiting until you are "ready" or "confident" to make a change? Maybe there is no such thing as ready. When are you ever really ready for what life hands you? Think about it—did you really feel ready for your last promotion, the house you bought, or the Ph.D. program you began? Certainly there are things you can do to be prepared, but maybe being ready is just a matter of declaring, "I'm ready." Tell yourself this, and then live as if it were true. Eventually, your feelings will catch up with your declaration.

As for confidence, nothing will increase your confidence more than *doing*. Thinking, analyzing, or obsessing about what you need to do will never make you feel more confident. In fact, it is usually the reverse. Life is like learning to ride a bicycle: you just need to get up and do anything new again and again until you feel confident. June is someone who was scared and lacked confidence but took action anyway, with great results.

From sociology to business

I first met June at a human relations training center, where she was leading workshops. At that time, she had a Ph.D. degree in sociology and was teaching at a major university. But over many years, on her vacations and in her spare time, she had steeped herself in her first love, diversity training. She attended classes in this area, read about the subject voraciously, and received training as a facilitator.

June attended my career workshop after many years of living this dual life. She was already pretty far along on her new career path. She had connected with a team of consultants and on her vacations she was co-leading training sessions within companies. She was also enrolled in a training program in organization development.

June knew it was time for her to leave the university. Very little of her interest or energy was there anymore. And yet she was loyal and also scared to leave. She was divorced and the mother of two daughters who were approaching college age. If she left, she would be turning her back on her Ph.D. degree, an established career, and a guaranteed paycheck. She would be stepping into self-employment and uncertainty. She didn't have a degree in her desired field and didn't know whether she was ready to declare herself a consultant. During the career workshop, I pointed out to June that she had been preparing for the transition for years, other people clearly saw her as ready, and her services were timely and valued by companies. On the Monday after the workshop, June announced to her dean that she would be leaving the university at the end of the year.

June has now been working full-time as a consultant for many years. In her first year on her own, she doubled her university salary. She has consistently exceeded those initial earnings and has never been without work for an extended period, just long enough to rest and relax. Her daughters have completed college, and June is an acknowledged expert in diversity training. She has worked for Fortune 500 companies with a highly respected team of professional consultants. When I ask her how it's going, she answers, "I'm out here doing God's work." Not only is she happy; she's also fulfilled because she is making a difference in an area she cares deeply about. ●

Women often use weight problems as an excuse for not taking some long-desired action. Prejudice about heavy people is a reality. My friend Susan worked for a leading computer manufacturer for more than twenty years and was not promoted into management even though she did the work of three people. She told me, "One day, I looked around and didn't see anyone else in top management who looked like me, a short, fat, middle-aged lady, and I knew there was no chance, so I gave up hope." (On the other hand, since leaving the company, Susan has found work that she truly loves. She is teaching at a business college, where she is appreciated and valued.) And then there's Vivian, who has had a weight problem for as long as I have known her but has never let it stop her. In fact, she leads aerobic classes for plus-size women, dressed in a leotard. So remember, weight is only an excuse. If there's anything you tell yourself you would do if you were twenty or more pounds lighter, start doing it now.

The list of things that can stop you is long. The point is, regardless of your reasons, just get started somewhere. Begin with the step you have the most energy for, and then let that lead you to what's next:

- Take action on that business idea you have had for so long.

- Have lunch with that person in your company who is doing work that intrigues you.

- Tell someone your dream—say it out loud.

- Volunteer in an area you would like to explore.

- Spend time with people who are doing what you are interested in doing.

- Tell your boss what you really want to do.

Jeff, a technical trainer, was sure his boss would think badly of him if he told him that he really wanted to work on change management. However, with my encouragement, he finally did so. He began by referring to a project on change he had successfully led six months earlier; then he said that ever since that time, he had known that change management was what he wanted to do. His boss responded by saying, "I've wondered why you didn't say something about it six months ago." Jeff is now very relieved to have his true feelings out in the open, and he and his boss are trying to figure out how he can do change management work and stay with the company. If you are unhappy at work, take a lesson from Jeff's experience. You may think you're hiding your discontent, but you aren't. The people around you will not be surprised when you tell them the truth.

Many clients tell me they have made requests at work when in fact they have not. If you are whining, pouting, complaining, or sulking, you are not making a request. It takes some rigor to make a request. First, you have to be clear about what you want, and then you have to state your wishes so other people understand them, too. Like a bewildered husband who has just heard the vague complaint "Honey, you don't love me," a manager can't respond to "I don't feel appreciated." Clarify what you want, and then ask for it.

Here are a few more action steps to get yourself moving:

- Update your résumé.

- Set up an informational interview.

- Read that book you've been eyeing about the field of work you're interested in.

- Take that computer, painting, or writing class you've been thinking about.

Just *do something, one something.* One step will lead to another, and before you know it, the paralysis will be lifted. One of my favorite sayings, which I had up on my office wall for years, is "This life is not a real life. It is just a test. Had it been a real life, you would have been told where to go and what to do." Stop waiting. Get into action. This just might be the real life.

You don't have to terrify yourself

Sometimes inaction is due to a trancelike hope, and sometimes it is due to fear. Many of my clients describe themselves as "stuck" when they first come to see me. When we look underneath the word, what surfaces is fear.

Perhaps you know what it is you want to do. You have listened to your heart and you see the steps you need to take, but you can't seem to do anything about it. The thought of leaving your current job, for instance, and stepping into the unknown is terrifying. What do you do? Begin by getting all your fears out on the table. Ask yourself, What am I afraid of? What's the worst thing that could happen to me if I pursue this path? Usually, just acknowledging your fears reduces the emotion surrounding them. You begin to see that they are greatly magnified or that there is something you can do about them.

I have found that fears about money are best handled on paper. Write down all your debts, all your assets, and the minimum amount of money you need to live on. Then break that down into months, weeks, days, and hours. For example, let's say you discover you need an income of $3,000 per month to pay your bills (excluding any luxuries) and cover taxes. That means you will need $36,000 per year. It sounds like a lot of money to earn, but now let's break it down: $3,000 per month is about $750 per week, which is $150 per day, or $18.75 per hour. You will probably have many more ideas about how to earn $18.75 per hour or $150 per day than about how to earn $36,000 per year. Annual income figures can sound overwhelming at first if you have always been in a salaried situation.

Unless you are someone who thrives on risk, be respectful of the fear you feel and be kind to yourself. You don't need to terrify yourself. Jumping into the abyss may not be the answer. Go after your dreams in a way that takes care of you. Take little steps, perhaps, as Dave did.

Dave becomes a writer

When Dave attended my career workshop, he was unhappy as a practicing architect. Deep inside, he had always wanted to be a writer, but he had not pursued writing because he couldn't see how he could make a living at it, especially as a fiction writer. After all, he had heard all the stories about starving writers.

During the workshop, Dave made the commitment to *be* a writer and pursue writing full out. He put writing first and then designed the rest of his life around it. Instead of quitting his job and stepping out with nothing except his writing, he resigned from his full-time job but negotiated part-time work with the same firm, just enough hours to allow him to support himself and write.

Dave took care of his survival needs and gave himself the time he needed to write. He began working on a series of historical novels. He has now had two books published and is working on his third. ●

If you need to continue working full-time, maybe all you can do right now is take a class, participate in a seminar, volunteer, or associate with people who are doing what you want to do. That's okay. Start anywhere. Anything you do, any step you take toward work you can put your heart into, will help you move from feeling victimized to feeling empowered.

I have noticed that for some reason, people even as young as thirty worry about "getting it right." They have the idea that there is one right answer to their work dilemmas. I don't agree. I think there are many possible ways to express our passions and talents in work. Nor is it true that if you don't get it right the first time you try, it's all over. I know otherwise. I have seen lots of people fail in their jobs at some time in their work life. Even being fired, put on probation, or passed over for promotion doesn't mean that you will never succeed or that there is something wrong with you. I have seen people go directly from failing at one job to succeeding at another, with no therapy in between. The problem is usually a wrong fit, not a deeply rooted personality disorder. Gina's experience is a good example.

From failure to success

Gina was referred to my career workshop by a colleague who had been working with her and was frustrated by her lack of progress. Gina had flunked out of medical school and was embarrassed, depressed, and confused about what to do next. Although she was very bright, she seemed to have few skills and was one of the most socially awkward people I had ever met. She constantly blinked her eyes, scowled, and twitched. She looked angry and strange. I wondered what in the world I could do to help her.

Over many months, though, a different person was revealed: a sweet, shy, introverted woman who loved anthropology. I finally asked Gina whether she was aware that she put people off with her behavior and, if so, why she did it. She admitted that she had started acting that way when she was young and afraid of some kids in her neighborhood. She said that when she acted "crazy" they didn't bother her and she felt safe. She agreed that this behavior did not work well for her as an adult and began working hard to change it.

In the meantime, Gina decided to focus on finding work that involved anthropology. Even though she knew a tremendous amount about the subject, she lacked an advanced degree in it or work experience, so she began by getting an internship at a local museum. Then she worked in a bookstore (a great place for someone who is introverted and shy) while she applied to museums across the United States. She was very persistent and thorough in her job search and did not get discouraged easily. Almost a year later, she landed a job in a museum and moved across the country. Letters from Gina expressed how much she loved her work. She had found a perfect fit and was now experiencing success. ●

Gina is an example of someone who didn't get it right the first time but was then able to create success for herself by telling the truth about where her passion was, getting into action, and following her heart. You don't have to get it right the first time, either. Just own the situation you're in and then do something about it. Don't be a victim or give up your power; just get into action.

key 1	Reveal what's true for you
key 2	Reclaim your personal power
key 3	Express your commitment
key 4	Surround yourself with support

Questions to ask yourself

- What am I waiting for?
- What is one step I can take that I have the energy for?
- If I weren't afraid, what would I do?

Action steps to take

*   If you can't change anything related to your job right now, begin by changing your hairstyle or the way you dress. If you need help, get support from experts.

*   Create space in your life for new things to enter by cleaning your closets and drawers. Create space in your mind by clearing your desk.

*   Do something entirely new and different that feels a little risky or out of the ordinary for you: go on rides at an amusement park; take skydiving lessons; eat at a restaurant alone; take an improvisation class.

Hang in there. You're on the right roller coaster.

—my friend who runs several
   successful businesses

chapter 4
key #3: express your commitment

We are often reluctant to commit ourselves to a job, project, or direction. We may pursue several different things simultaneously, saying, "I need lots of options," " I want to leave the door open," or "It's smart to have something to fall back on." These are all common sayings and typical of what friends and family members will tell you to do, but they are dangerous advice. When we are focused and committed, we produce results. When we aren't, we diffuse our energies and confuse people about what we want.

If you go off in several different directions, you will abort your own attempts to build a powerful network. Conducting a successful job search is largely a matter of building a strong network of people who can provide information about an industry, lead you to resources, give you the "scoop" on working for particular companies and people, and let you know about leads for job openings.

If you are looking for work in two or three different arenas at the same time, you will have to build a different network for each one, none of which will probably end up being well developed, and the people around you will not be able to keep in mind what you really want.

It's no different if you decide to start a business. Any good business is built almost entirely on its reputation, long before advertising has any effect. If you are not committed to your business, your customers will definitely know it. All you have to do is go into a store that has an absentee owner to experience the effects of a lack of commitment. The merchandise is not special and is sloppily displayed. The salespeople who wait on you are uninformed and disinterested. Spirit and energy are missing.

Projects won't get off the ground if you are not committed because the other people involved in them will reflect your half-hearted efforts. Putting yourself on the line can feel scary, but as soon as you make a commitment, you can use the energy in that fear to get to work and start producing results.

Take the high road

How serious are you about your career? Use the following scale to measure your commitment to your current job or to a recent decision—for example, to explore a new direction, leave or stay with your company, launch a business of your own, start a project, or go back to school.

0	5	10
I'm interested	I'm trying	I'm committed

What do you need to do in order to be a 10? Maybe you just need to declare your commitment and act from that. Making a commitment is taking the high road. You may be resisting commitment to a career path, a direction in a job search, or even to a project because you think the commitment will limit you, but in fact just the opposite is true. Making a commitment is freeing. Just think about any decision over which you have agonized for a period of time:

- Which college should I attend?

- Do I want to buy the white house with the great backyard or the red brick house with the fireplace?

- Is this the time to move to California, as I've always wanted to do, or should I stay here with all my friends and family?

- Should I stay in sales or try something new?

- Am I ready for a promotion?

Now remember how you felt once you made the decision. You were probably filled with relief, brimming with creative ideas about how to make it work, and inspired to get on with your life. Here's what happened to Marcia when she made a commitment.

Marcia's business

Marcia was suffering from indecision when she attended my career workshop. Five years before, she had started an employment agency that placed pharmacists in temporary assignments, but the business was just limping along. Marcia was discouraged and knew she had to decide whether to stay with the business or do something else.

During her first summer out of pharmacy school, Marcia had been employed as a temporary worker and had really liked it. She had had small children at the time, and temp work had given her the flexibility to be with them more. But then she applied for a full-time job because she thought she "should." She worked for a year and became bored. She returned to temp work and noticed what it was that she liked about it: it was short-term, focused work with a lot of variety as well as a great deal of responsibility. She really had to concentrate at each new job, and she loved taking special care of someone else's territory because she felt trusted. She began getting more calls than she could handle, so she called in other pharmacists to fill positions. Because she was a natural networker, her business was quickly off and running.

I wondered why her business was not growing now. When I asked Marcia whether she would want to stay with her business if she could figure out a way to expand it, the answer was a strong yes. It was clearly where her heart was. It was perplexing, then, that she was not experiencing the success she wanted. When I explored further I discovered that while she was trying to build the business, Marcia was still filling temp jobs herself because she lacked confidence and thought she needed the security. The result was that she was dabbling in her business rather than giving it her all.

During the workshop, Marcia decided to go for it and made a full-out commitment to expand the business. She stopped filling temporary jobs herself and focused on placing other pharmacists. Now, more than ten years after the workshop, Marcia has placed pharmacists in thirty states, in both small pharmacies and large chains; has regular customers in fourteen states; has ten employees of her own, and runs a multimillion-dollar business. ●

Marcia's commitment has extended beyond her business, to the pharmacy industry as a whole. She has given speeches and championed causes and is fighting for simple improvements in the workplace for pharmacists, such as chairs to sit on and lunch breaks. Moreover, she is on the cutting edge of advances in the industry. Currently, she is training her temporary pharmacists to consult with patients about possible side effects of drugs and is advising owners of pharmacies on how to make them into educational centers for customers—for example, by providing information about diabetes management.

Marcia's success is a great example of what can happen when we stop dabbling and make a full commitment.

Decide what you are willing to put up with

Perhaps you are waiting to find the "perfect" job or work situation before you make a commitment. I am convinced that no job or work setting is perfect, no matter how glamorous it may be or how much we love it. Every job has negative aspects that come with the territory. Take advertising, for instance. Advertising work can be glamorous, fun, and extremely well paid. On the other hand, it can involve long hours and more travel than you might wish, and there can be a certain amount of insecurity: on Friday you may have a job and on Monday you may not. An account can be lost without warning, and there is no severance package. That's just the way it is. It comes with the territory.

Or think about having your own business. It's exciting to be your own boss and not answer to anyone except your customers.

You can create your business the way you want it to be. But the work never ends, there's no one else to blame for problems or mistakes, and the cash flow can be uneven and uncertain. All this also comes with the territory. In fact, something unpleasant or negative *always* comes with the territory. It isn't a matter of finding something without negatives; the question is, What are you willing to put up with? If you choose work that you love, it will be far easier to deal with the negatives than if you are doing work that you just fell into or that other people think you should do. Decide what you are willing to do or put up with, and then make your commitment.

Are you trying to figure out how you will accomplish your goals before you make a commitment to them? Are you looking for evidence that you are making the right decision? Do you tell people what you are thinking about and then listen for their reaction to help you decide what to do? The problem in doing this is that many people become skeptical and cautious when asked for advice. Moreover, their answer reflects how it would be for them, not for you. First make a commitment, and *then* figure out how you will carry it out.

Like many people, you may believe you can't afford to make a mistake in choosing a work direction at this point in your life. Don't worry. Once you start out on a new path, your life will never be the same anyway. Regardless of what happens, you will meet new people, have new experiences, and grow. And discovering that something is *not* right can be as empowering as finding what *is* right. It takes you further along the path to where your heart really is.

What do you do if you have so many interests you can't decide which one to pursue? Just choose. It almost doesn't matter what you choose; just choose *something* and get started. The rest will fall into place. Either you will decide you were wrong and this choice should remain a hobby, or your commitment will feel right and will grow. Choose the idea that keeps coming to mind again and again.

And as for all your other interests, think "both/and," not "either/or." There are ways to continue having them in your life. Perhaps they will be interests or hobbies, or you may pursue them later as other careers or combine them, as Peter did.

Peter's dream

Peter had been in advertising since he was very young. He began by working for small companies, and after several years he joined a large national agency, where he did very well. He was promoted and given increasing responsibility, recognition, and pay. By most measures, he should have been satisfied, but Peter had an unfulfilled personal goal that ate at the edges of his consciousness for years. He wanted to be a minister.

Peter experienced this yearning from the first time he began attending his church, years ago. By the time I met him, when he was in his mid-thirties, Peter was confused about his future and felt immobilized. He thought he would have to make a choice between the ministry and the business world, and yet he was interested in both. And he was quite sure he did not want to have a parish of his own, especially since he had recently married, bought a house, and started a family. So, what to do?

When we began working together, Peter started exploring options and stopped suffering. He talked to people and investigated programs in theology as well as advertising and promotion work with nonprofit organizations. He got into action when he moved out of "either this or that" thinking and into "both/and." He found peace when he arrived at the conclusion that he wanted to bring "ministering" to whatever work he did.

Peter then took two major steps: he enrolled in classes on a part-time basis at a local theological school, and he volunteered at his advertising agency to head a program to provide pro bono work for nonprofit organizations. Peter now has a clear vision of using the power of business and advertising to help nonprofit organizations. He is fulfilling his dream of "ministering" right where he is. ●

Match your actions with your words

After clarifying what you are committed to, your next step is to coordinate your actions with your commitments. When I first started my business, I was working alone, out of my home. It was really difficult. I was often lonely and was struggling with selling my services. Whenever I got a string of no's, which happened pretty often, I would go into a slump and become depressed. In the beginning, these periods of depression lasted a long time, sometimes days. I thought there was nothing I could do except wait them out. One day, however, I discovered that I could be depressed and pick up the telephone and sell anyway. It was a real breakthrough for me and very empowering. On that day, I was coordinating my actions with my commitment to something bigger than my feelings. It is powerful to create a distinction between how we feel about something and what we are committed to.

Stick with it

Another way to express your commitment is to stick with your dreams and goals, to refuse to give up, to do whatever it takes to make them a reality. Robert is someone who did just that.

Flying high

For as long as he could remember, Robert had wanted to be a pilot. He studied hard and got his pilot's license and then applied for work repeatedly at major airlines. He was rejected every time. When he came to me for help, he was pretty discouraged and wondered what else he should do for a career.

After he attended my career workshop, Robert was inspired and reestablished his goal of becoming a professional pilot. He decided he wouldn't give up. He enrolled in more flying classes to rekindle his passion, sharpen his skills, and earn instructor status. Then he began knocking on doors again. This time, he decided to start with smaller companies and apply as a corporate pilot. He identified one company he really liked, and every week for a couple of months he stopped by to see whether there was an opening.

One day, there was. A pilot had left suddenly, and the company needed someone as soon as possible. Because the owners already knew Robert, he had been persistent, and he was in the right place at the right time, he was hired immediately. He has begun flying and believes he is getting great experience. When he's ready, he'll apply to the major airlines again, this time with a good track record already in place. ●

I love Robert's story of how he didn't give up and his persistence paid off. I also love the story I heard from a client who told me it had taken him eight years to get his college degree while working full-time to support himself, his wife, and their two children. He admitted it had been hard but expressed satisfaction at having done it "on his own time and his own dime." He was recently promoted to a management position at his company and is now considering graduate school. If he does begin graduate school, I know he will finish because he knows how to stick with it until he gets the prize.

As you continue to pursue the goal of creating satisfying work and a life you love, it is important to remember that making a commitment is not a onetime event. You will need to renew your commitment again and again. Life is not static. You will encounter new obstacles; get tired, bored, or discouraged; occasionally lose your way or get sidetracked; grow up and grow old; notice that your energy and priorities have changed; and even discard some values and adopt new ones. So remember that commitment needs to be ongoing. Committing yourself to work is no different from committing yourself to any important relationship or undertaking. From time to time you need to reevaluate your decison and then renew your commitment, or commit yourself to a new direction.

	key 1	Reveal what's true for you
	key 2	Reclaim your personal power
	key 3	Express your commitment
	key 4	Surround yourself with support

Questions to ask yourself

- On a scale of 1 to 10, with 1 being "just enough to show up each day" and 10 being "full-out, body and soul," how committed am I to my current work? What is needed to make it a 10?

- If I am not committed to my current work, what could I be committed to?

- Am I willing to do the things I don't like doing as well as the things I love doing in order to be successful?

Action steps to take

- Use the word *committed* when you talk, instead of words such as *want, wish,* or *would like to;* for example, "I am committed to expanding my business" or "I am committed to going to school." Experience your sense of commitment in your body as you say the words.

- Take any one thing in your life about which you are being indecisive and make a decision about it, even if you hear internal voices saying, "But what about . . . ?" Just decide.

- Establish a time frame for your commitment to a new direction—for example, tell yourself, "I'll do this for one year and then reevaluate my commitment." Just be sure the time you allot is enough to allow for some success.

Don't stop! Keep going! You can do it!

—cheers from my ropes course team
that echo in my mind years later

chapter 5
key #4: surround yourself with support

Today, with the support I have available to me, I can get away with wallowing in fear or self-pity for about fifteen minutes. I spent whole days or even weeks wallowing when I first started my business. How about you? Do you have the support you need to help keep you on your path?

Retire your internal Lone Ranger

Although independence is one goal to achieve in growing up, it is not the ultimate goal. Interdependence is a higher form of maturity. By focusing only on independence, not only do we create competition within our companies instead of directing it, more appropriately, at our companies' competitors, but we also create work environments in which people would rather fail than ask for help. I have worked with clients who were in over their heads at work and desperately needed help but were afraid to ask for it, especially if they were members of a minority group. They were convinced that any request for help would be viewed as a sign of weakness or an indication that they were "not cutting it." Not only does this perpetuate a painful work environment, but it's also a counterproductive way to work. It limits the potential of everyone.

It is particularly damaging to avoid asking for help when we are unemployed. I remember a few clients who were not making any progress in their job search even though they were clear about what they wanted and were eager to work. For a while, I was stumped. Finally, they confessed that they were not networking and, in fact, had not told anyone about being unemployed because they were ashamed. Two of them revealed that they had not even told their families. They wanted to keep their layoff a secret until they were close to being hired again. This is needlessly isolating and cuts out the people who are probably most willing to help.

When we are in high school and/or college, we have a lot of support around us naturally. After we leave school, it is up to us to create the support we need, and this includes being discerning about what we read and listen to every day. Of course, it is important to be aware of what is happening in the world, but the news media present an extremely unbalanced and negative view of life. It is equally important to keep feeding our dreams and visions. It is our job to inspire ourselves—to read inspiring books and articles and to listen to motivating tapes and CDs. People who are in sales are ahead of the pack when it comes to these habits. They fill their heads with inspiration instead of gloom and doom. We need to learn from them.

Although it is not impossible, it is very difficult to succeed in your ideal work life if your spouse, roommate, lover, family, friends, or co-workers are not supportive of your goals. We all feel vulnerable when we have a new dream, and even casual comments from those closest to us can set us back. At such times, it may be necessary to reduce the amount of time you spend with some of the important people in your life until you feel strong enough to stand up for your choices in their presence. You may even have to retrain some people because in the past you have colluded with their negativity and let them get away with it. Ask them not to say anything negative or request that they support you in specific ways. You may have to leave your old neighborhood to fulfill your dreams; otherwise, you will feel as if you are swimming upstream. But what will probably happen when you take a stand for your dreams is that the people around you will, too. After a while, some of those who initially voiced the most skepticism (such as parents) may become your greatest supporters. It's up to you to enroll them.

Surrounding yourself with support is a way to ensure your success; it's like setting up a safety net. If you have enough support around you, it will be almost impossible for you to fail. We all have times when we get discouraged or question ourselves. I don't believe that success comes automatically just because we are clear about what we want to do. That is only the first step. It takes a lot of hard work to succeed, even with work we love, and there are often setbacks, disappointments, and failures along the way.

A group that meets regularly can be one form of support. Such a group provides a structure for fulfilling your dreams by keeping them "on the front burner." If you don't have a group to join, form your own, as Marcy did.

Support for an artist

Marcy runs a technical writing business from her home. Even though she had been successfully self-employed for five years when she attended my workshop, she was unhappy and feeling restless. Marcy was grateful for her success, but her work was mainly repetitive, tedious, and uninteresting. After the workshop, she joined my monthly entrepreneurs' group for support in expanding her business, thinking that would relieve her boredom.

In the entrepreneurs' group, Marcy revealed that she had never thought of herself as an artist but was yearning to express herself more artistically. We encouraged her to start acting like an artist right away and to fill her life with art. She began by taking drawing and painting classes. She brought samples to meetings to show us her progress and to keep herself productive. In addition, she formed an artists' group with a jeweler, a writer, a painter, and a potter. The group meets each month to share ideas and inspiration about art and to stimulate creativity. Members are clear that it is not a group to share sad stories about how bad it is for artists.

Another idea that came from the entrepreneurs' group was for Marcy to start delegating some of the work that she has outgrown. Marcy is happier in her business now because she is moving toward her new goal of becoming a full-time illustrator. She is experimenting with taking on more creative assignments in her business and is actively feeding her creative spirit outside of work. Both the artists' and entrepreneurs' support groups have contributed to her growth. ●

People provide the most important form of support, but physical environments are also important. Most of us are not very conscious of our work environment. We don't even notice that our desk is a mess, the walls need painting, the filing cabinets are stuffed to the gills and the drawers are hard to open, and there is nothing inspiring on the walls. We may be surrounded by relics of the past as if we were frozen in a bygone era. Most offices are sterile or drab at best, and yet we yearn to be creative. Our environment says a lot about how seriously we are pursuing our dreams. It either supports our work or hinders it, as Teri's experience illustrates.

Taking it seriously

I met Teri three years after she joined a multilevel marketing organization that sold cookware through home parties. It was a well-established, successful company with a high level of integrity and good opportunities for growth. Teri thought this work was perfect for her because she loved the products and loved working from home (she had two small children, to whom she wanted to be close). She also enjoyed earning extra money for the household and learning such skills as speaking in front of groups.

Teri requested help from me because she was doing "just okay" and wanted to do better. I was interested in whether she valued her work and discovered that this was the place we needed to start. Teri had fallen into the habit of agreeing with her husband that her work was a "cute little hobby," as he put it, instead of valuing it as a serious business with good potential. I encouraged Teri to set daily and weekly goals and, even more important, to work on changing the attitudes and behavior of family members.

One of the most important things Teri did was carve out a working space for herself that was off-limits to everyone else. She no longer allowed her children and husband to drop on her desk whatever they had in their hands. It became a true work space. As Teri began to take her work more seriously, everyone

around her did, too. And, of course, as she managed her work
life better, her sales improved and more money came in. Gradually, her husband became one of her biggest supporters. •

Unfortunately, the vast majority of people do not have a positive attitude about work. Their conversations are full of complaints
and expressions such as "Thank God it's Friday" or "It's blue Monday." The tone may be kidding, but the problem is that we do not
leave such conversations feeling uplifted. In fact, we usually have
to pick ourselves up off the floor and pump ourselves up to get
started again. These conversations create a dreary work environment and make it difficult for us to express genuine excitement
about our work. By participating in such exchanges in hallways,
rest rooms, and lunchrooms during the working day, and in bars
after work, we become a member of the "Ain't it awful?" club.
Instead, what most of us really need at work is a "Hallelujah chorus," a group of people who will challenge us to keep pursuing our
dreams, who will remind us of what we want for ourselves when we
have forgotten, and who see us bigger than we see ourselves in
moments when we feel small.

Put it on a treasure map

One of the best things you can do to support your dreams and goals
is to create a treasure map, a visual display of them. It is an idea I
learned from Catherine Ponder, who has written many books about
creating prosperity. I have been giving this assignment to clients for
many years, and I often meet people on the street who say to me,
"You know that treasure map we made in the workshop? I've got
everything I put on it!"

Making a treasure map is particularly useful if you are feeling
stuck in picturing your future. Your dreams can be obscured by your

concerns or by competing thoughts. Visualizing your dreams and choosing pictures that represent them brings you in touch with your unconscious mind and makes the dreams more accessible.

I like treasure maps because they are a reminder to incorporate all aspects of your life when working on your career goals, since work is always intertwined with everything else. The pictures allow you to integrate the different parts of your life. Here's how to work on your treasure map.

Making your treasure map

Begin by taking some quiet time alone. Relax your entire body, from your head to your toes. Do this by telling all your muscles to relax. Begin with those in your face and work down to your neck, shoulders, back, arms, hands, stomach, buttocks, legs, feet, and toes. Then sit quietly for a minute and notice the evenness of your breathing and how relaxed your whole body feels. Now picture what would be an ideal day for you three to five years from now. In every part of your life, see yourself as confident, happy, full of energy, and enthusiastic.

Begin with waking up in the morning. Where are you living—in a house, apartment, or condominium? In the country, a city, or a suburb? Who else is there, or have you chosen to live alone? Don't forget to include pets if you want them. Look around your home. See yourself get up and get dressed for work. Carry out your favorite early morning rituals.

Now go to work. Where do you go? How are you dressed? See yourself at work doing what you most love to do, surrounded by people or alone. What are you working on? (Make sure it's exciting and challenging.) What are the people around you doing? How much money do you make?

Now come to the end of your workday and do what you would enjoy most—being with the children? Playing or relaxing in other ways? Finally, as you end the day, reflect with satisfaction on all you had to do to get where you are now, all the steps and the risks you had to take, and give thanks for your blessings.

When you have completed this visualization, either write down your goals first and then make your treasure map or make your treasure map and then write down your goals. The sequence doesn't matter; do whatever works best for you. When you write down your goals, work backward, from five years to three years, one year, six months, three months, one month. To make your treasure map, get some poster board or any other sturdy material. It can be any color you choose. I recommend that you begin with at least a standard-size poster board so that you will think big. Later, when you are more accustomed to dreaming, you can make smaller treasure maps. Cut out pictures and words from magazines and brochures to represent goals in all areas of your life—relationships, travel, recreation, health, physical fitness, money, work, play, spirituality, material possessions. Begin by cutting out those images and words that "speak" to you in some way. Don't try to figure out why you are drawn to them; just cut them out. Paste them on the poster board. Use more pictures than words—they're more powerful, and the images will become a part of you. Be sure to add a picture of yourself. Have fun and be creative. Add symbols if you want to, and make your treasure map in any shape that pleases you. For example, one client traced her body and turned that into her treasure map; another did hers as a cylinder; and a third did it as a book.

Making a treasure map is a powerful exercise. Your choices will come from your unconscious mind; you may notice that your hand seems to select certain pictures or words of its own accord. Your thoughts will be clarified as you work, and you will experience the act of making a commitment as you paste the pictures onto the poster board.

Catherine Ponder suggests that when you have completed your treasure map you should place it where you can see it every day until you are tired of it. Then put it away. You will have internalized it, and it will serve as a clear picture of what you want in the future. This is a process you can repeat whenever you want. Some people update their map each year; others make new ones.

Your treasure map is very revealing. It speaks loudly about who you are, what you want, what's important to you, and what's missing in your life right now. I remember one client who had *nothing* about work on her treasure map. After a good laugh, we worked with the "princess" part of her who wanted to be taken care of, exploring what that was all about.

Your treasure map may reveal an imbalance in your life—for example, all work and no play, an absence of relationships, or the need to enrich your life with more interests. Sometimes it becomes clear that a relationship, not work, is your major goal. That's okay, of course, and such a revelation is important. My personal opinion, however, from having spent much of my adult life single, is that doing work you love is the best antidote for loneliness and increases your odds of being a good companion. After all, who wants to spend time with someone who hates his or her work and complains about it all the time? Sometimes treasure maps are cluttered, reflecting a need for simplicity, or are rigid or bleak, like the one a client did all in black and white, mostly newsprint. Would it surprise you to know that this was a man who needed to include his heart more in his work and life? Your treasure map can be a tool for gaining insight into yourself. The more you and your trusted friends look at it, the more you will learn.

Be sure to include only positive words on your map. For example, don't use phrases such as "End war." You don't want to look at your treasure map and see the word *war*. It's better to use words such as *peace* and *harmony*. You will never be sorry you took the time to do this exercise. And you can do it again year after year.

Handle the demons inside

I recently talked to a client who confided to me, "I'm my own worst enemy." We're usually our own harshest critics and the first to question our own abilities. Most of us have a chorus of taunting voices inside our head: "What makes you think you can do this?" "Who do you think you are?" "What about the last time you tried to do this and failed?" "What will Mom (or Dad) say?" "You'll never make any money at it." "You're too old." "It's too late." When people around us voice these same concerns, it's like hearing our own mind on a loudspeaker. There is no way to silence your doubts completely. They'll always be there, but the best way to turn down the volume is to get into action and surround yourself with support. You can even learn to welcome the doubting voices of others as an opportunity to stand up for yourself and practice speaking up powerfully for your dreams. Marie is someone who used support to accomplish a long-held dream.

Marie's dream

Marie was in her eighteenth year of work for a computer sales company and was close to celebrating her fortieth birthday when she came to me for help. She was unhappy and felt stressed in her work, but primarily she was upset with herself because she had wanted to go to graduate school for years but something had always gotten in the way. Usually, it was work.

Marie had to travel a lot in her job and was afraid she would miss too many classes. There was also the problem of money, and she had doubts about whether she would be accepted, questioned why she wanted a graduate degree in the first place, didn't see how she could afford it, and so on.

After clarifying that a master's degree in journalism was what she wanted, Marie joined my support group and began putting the pieces in place. At work, she asked for and received a transfer to a position that was less stressful and required very little travel. Then she researched schools, chose one, took classes to prepare for the graduate record exam, studied during lunch hours and weekends, took the exam, completed the applications, scaled down her lifestyle ("Where was all that money going?"), and saved money to pay her way through school. When I last spoke to Marie, she had been accepted and planned to attend classes the following semester. In the three months left before school began, she planned to take a trip to Europe, go on a spiritual retreat, and finish up some volunteer projects. She was "getting her house in order," and by the start of the semester, she would be ready for school. This time, nothing would stop her. ●

Revealing the truth to ourselves sometimes leads us to leave our present situation and sometimes rekindles our commitment to stay. If you are beginning to suspect that the only way for you to find satisfying work and a life you love is to leave, first read Part Two and learn how to apply the four keys to finding fulfillment at work where you are right now. Take all the steps to become empowered in your current work setting, and who knows? Maybe you will decide it is the best place to be after all.

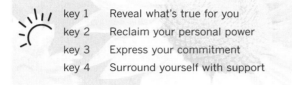

key 1   Reveal what's true for you
key 2   Reclaim your personal power
key 3   Express your commitment
key 4   Surround yourself with support

Questions to ask yourself

- Do I have people around me who are willing to be straight-forward and confront me if necessary?

- Who already knows about my dreams? What other trust-worthy people do I need to tell?

- If I can't find an existing support group, how can I go about creating one?

Action steps to take

- Look around your office or work space. Is it inspiring, moti-vating, at least minimally pleasant, or peaceful? If not, do what-ever you can to change it.

- Buy some inspiring tapes or CDs and listen to them. Bookstores are full of them, and there are companies that specialize in marketing motivational tapes. Nightingale-Conant Corpora-tion, in Niles, Illinois, is one of them.

- Find at least one other person to enlist as a partner. Work with your partner to set goals, report results regularly, and keep each other on track.

- Don't listen to news broadcasts or read newspapers more than once or twice a week—read something inspiring instead.

part two

if you decide to stay

When I went back to work after the workshop,
everyone had changed. They were so great.
I wondered what had happened to them.

—many graduates of my career workshop

chapter 6
first, alter your relationship to work

"Heaven" might be attainable right where you are. Maybe it has little to do with where you work and everything to do with your attitude about work and the way you manage yourself. If you decide to stay with your current employer, start by altering your relationship to work.

As is the case for most people, your thoughts about work may be depressing and disempowering. Do you hold any of the following views of work?

- Work is a prison sentence.
- The workplace is a war zone.
- The most important thing at work is to get ahead.

You have the power to decide how you want work to be in your life. You can create a different context for work from the ones just described. How about the following instead?

Work is a gift. We often think that what we really want is not to have to work, but anyone who has been unemployed for very long quickly begins to appreciate working. Doing nothing is appealing only when we're overtired or for short periods of time. Otherwise, we miss the focus that work provides. It is an organizing principle for the other parts of our life. We miss having somewhere to go, being productive and useful, having a place to contribute our talents and skills, having something to be proud of, the camaraderie of co-workers or customers, and the rewards (achievements, money, etc.) work brings. Instead of having to push unemployed clients back to work, I usually have to encourage them to slow down and not rush into the next job. It's natural for human beings to engage in some form of work. This may take the form of a part-time job, a business run from the home, the job of raising children, or volunteer work. Even if you have no choice about working, remember that you can choose your job and the way you do it.

The workplace provides an unparalleled opportunity for self-expression and personal growth and development. We are constantly challenged at work to be at our best. This challenge gives us an opportunity to discover our gifts. It also demands that we continue to mature as individuals and develop our talents.

The most important thing is to find interesting and challenging work. Getting to the "top" is a myth for the vast majority of people. It always has been. There has never been room at the top level for large numbers of people because most companies are designed as pyramids. And now that organizations are being downsized, "rightsized," and flattened, there are even fewer opportunities to climb the ladder to the top; even the ladder is being removed.

---

chart 2
the ten key qualities of self-development

1. Courage
2. Empathy
3. Commitment
4. Openness
5. Responsibility
6. Flexibility
7. Authenticity
8. Integrity
9. Resourcefulness
10. Generativity

This may not be as bad as it looks initially. Climbing the corporate ladder has traditionally meant being promoted to a managerial position, and this has posed a big problem for many people. I work with many unhappy managers who feel far removed from the work they once loved and were good at. They lack the skills to be good managers and, in truth, are not even interested in the role. The problem is that the only way we know how to reward our stars is to make them managers, and yet the job of a manager is to make stars out of others. For most people, it is a difficult transition at best. A promotion may end up being a detriment. So it is much healthier and more promising to focus on having interesting and challenging work than on getting ahead. Chart 2 presents the ten qualities I have found to be crucial to successful self-development. Assessment 2 will help you weigh the factors affecting your decision to stay in or leave your present work situation.

assessment 2
where are you on the scales?

Check only those statements that are true for you right now.

Stay?	Leave?
___ I love the company and what it stands for—it has integrity.	___ I'm disgusted by the policies, politics, or practices where I work.
___ I see lots of opportunity in the future to grow and learn.	___ I'm not challenged. There's nothing else to do here that will allow me to learn and grow.
___ I'm using all my talents in my work.	___ The only real reason I'm staying is that I'm scared to go.
___ I think I can make a difference here.	___ I've tried everything to make it better, but nothing works.
___ I'm optimistic about my opportunities here.	___ I don't see a future for myself here.
___ I like the atmosphere and feel comfortable here.	___ The company is no longer what I signed on with; I don't like it anymore.
___ I'm included and involved in decision making.	___ I'm increasingly left out of things.
___ I feel respected and appreciated.	___ No matter what I do, I am not listened to or taken seriously.
___ It's fun to work here.	___ I yearn for more freedom, more time, or a different work situation or lifestyle.
___ This is an emotionally healthy and fair work environment.	___ I have physical symptoms related to how stressed and unhappy I am at work (headaches, back pain, etc.).
___ I have a great job with a great title.	___ It's clear that I'll never get where I want to go in this company.

Stay?	Leave?
___ I work hard, but I have a full life outside of work.	___ I work too many hours and have no life outside of work.
___ I have a great relationship with my boss.	___ I have a very bad relationship with my boss, and he or she is here to stay.
___ My boss is not a workaholic and is a good role model.	___ My boss is abusive and insulting.
___ I respect people I work with.	___ I don't respect my co-workers.
___ My co-workers are helpful and collaborative.	___ I made a mistake in the past and no one seems to be able to forget it.
___ I feel that I can be myself here.	___ I don't fit in here—I'm like a square peg in a round hole.
___ I feel very challenged by and interested in my work.	___ My work does not interest me.
___ I'm as interested in my work as I am in my hobbies.	___ I have more energy for, interest in, and enjoyment with my hobbies or small business outside of work than I do with my job.
___ I earn enough or more than enough.	___ I'm unhappy about my pay. I think I'm worth much more and am not paid fairly.

Total score:_____   Total score:_____

Are the scales clearly tipped? Of course, you can't make such an emotional, important, and often painful decision as deciding to leave or stay in a job just by the numbers, and some statements will have more importance for you than others. But did this exercise reveal anything? For example, when the negatives outweigh the positives, it's easier to decide to go. But when the scores are more evenly balanced, it's harder. That's when it's especially important to give it everything you've got at work before deciding to leave.

Remember: it's your life, and you're in charge

At some point after clients have complained for a while about their work, I inevitably end up telling them that they sound like victims. They usually respond in a surprised tone of voice, "I do, don't I?" It's easy to forget that you're in charge of your own work situation and life. But if you remind yourself that you are in charge and then act in ways that are consistent with that belief, you will create great results. Shift your attention away from "they" and "them" and away from strategizing about how to get ahead. Instead, focus on developing the following ten qualities in yourself.

Courage

Courage is the most important of the ten key qualities of self-development. It is the foundation for all the others. There are opportunities every day at work to demonstrate courage. For one person, it might take courage to voice a dissenting opinion or speak up in a meeting. For another, it might take courage to try something new. I am reminded of Elizabeth.

Out on her own

Elizabeth was forty years old and had worked at a low-level secretarial job for fifteen years. She had great difficulty expressing herself verbally. At our first meeting, she couldn't express what she wanted or really even why she had come to see me. She just knew she needed a change. I was not surprised when she missed her next appointment. I didn't hear from her for many months, and then her company expanded and new opportunities opened up. One of them was a secretarial job in a division located in Arizona.

Elizabeth sought me out again. Could I help her present herself well in an interview? She revealed that she had always wanted to move to Arizona and thought she could get this job. She told me she was determined to do this. She further revealed that moving from home would allow her to be out on her own and away from an overbearing and domineering mother for the first time ever. Elizabeth's eyes sparkled with excitement as she talked, and her hands shook with fear. It was an enormous step for her, requiring a great deal of courage.

She followed through, applied for the job, had a great interview, and was hired. When I met with Elizabeth to say good-bye, her face radiated a new level of confidence. "I did it," she said. ●

For some people, a job change and a move to another part of the country would not require courage, but disagreeing with the boss would. And for almost all of us, it takes courage to question whether our work is a good fit and we are in the right place, to listen to our heart, and to then take action.

Empathy

Good relationships are the "bottom line" of any successful work, including business transactions. The major skill we need to develop to cultivate good relationships is listening—listening for, to, and with. We must listen for other people's commitments, concerns, and enthusiasms; listen to what people are saying on the surface as well as to the music underneath; listen with full attention, apart from our own agenda, and with feeling for people's position, experience, and perspective. Listening in this way allows us to align ourselves with others, see their potential, hear what they are really saying, and awaken our own empathy and compassion. It also allows people to give us feedback, coaching, and ideas (without which we will fail). Learn to listen to input from everyone, not just from who *you* decide can give it to you. This includes listening to yourself and honoring your own needs.

Commitment

Most of us give up too easily. We allow ourselves to be stopped by other people's negative comments; we get hurt; we get discouraged; we lose confidence in ourselves or our ideas; we become overwhelmed by obstacles; we get sidetracked by diversions; we become cynical and give up on our hopes and visions. I have had the privilege of working with clients over long periods of time and have been able to follow what happens to many of them. Those who have demonstrated commitment and have persisted through thick and thin have been successful; those who have given up have not. Decide what you are committed to and then stick with it, but be clear about the distinction between commitment and attachment. None of us can afford to be attached to our job or company in light of the furious rate of change we confront today. But we can continue to be committed to our work, our values, and our goals and visions.

Openness

When we have invested time and energy in learning a certain way of doing something, it is hard to be open to another way. We become enthralled with our ideas and turn them into cherished beliefs. But the world is changing rapidly and dramatically, and we will not survive the changes if we are rigid. We can hold on to our standards while letting go of old ideas or ways of doing things. With diversity of age, background, culture, and gender becoming more the norm than the exception in the workplace, it is even more important for us to open our minds as well as our hearts.

Responsibility

Taking responsibility for the good stuff is easy. Taking it for the bad is hard, but it's a powerful stand to take and will enable you to move out of the victim role. It requires a major shift from pointing fingers and blaming everyone and everything else for your circumstances to "owning" the situation you are currently in, no matter how it looks. Ask yourself this: Given the circumstances, what do I need to do now?

Flexibility

When you begin pursuing your dreams, you can count on meeting obstacles, confronting unexpected developments, and finding that some things do not turn out the way you pictured them. Flexibility is a quality that will help you continue on your path without giving up your dream. You may, however, have to give up your expectations of exactly how your dream should develop and relax into another version of it. It is important to remind yourself that there are lots of ways to get there, not just one.

Authenticity

Do you put on a "work face" or assume a work persona when you go to work? If so, I guarantee that what you present at work is not the most alive or interesting you. The authentic you is far more interesting and vital. Putting on a "work face" is part of the reason for the trancelike state most people enter into at work. Acting with congruence between your inside and outside will allow you to experience a better energy flow and more inner peace in your life. And co-workers and customers will trust you more. We know when people are not being sincere, don't we? Something feels "off." It pays to bring the full *you* to work. Here's how Harry did it.

A comedian at work

Harry is a comedian on the inside and an accountant on the outside. When I met him, he felt trapped and unhappy. He wanted to be a comedian but didn't see how to do it. All he knew was accounting work. In the support group after the career workshop, we began challenging him to bring his gifts more openly to his current job. We told him to *be* a comedian right now, not yearn to be one sometime in the future. He began to express his humor more openly at work.

Now Harry creates funny telephone messages every day as a means of self-expression, and people call just to hear them. He is also writing humorous stories about his industry, which he knows well, and is beginning to be booked as a speaker. He lightens up meetings with funny comments. As a result of expressing himself more authentically and being appreciated by everyone around him, he is less resentful about work. At the same time, he is also more productive. And he is taking steps to create full-time work for himself as a humor writer and per-forming comedian. ●

Integrity

We all have an internal alarm system that lets us know when we are not acting with integrity. It's our job to listen to the alarm and honor it. Being out of touch with our integrity is like being out of sorts. Something is missing. Our outside actions don't match our inside intentions. Acting with integrity allows us to experience wholeness and completeness.

Resourcefulness

If you analyze the qualities you have used in your most fulfilling personal accomplishments, you will find resourcefulness often present. Yet in your work, you may not be using this quality. It is common when we are employed by a company to think someone else will or should provide all the resources we need to be successful in our job. The problem with this attitude is that it encourages us to operate from a sense of entitlement that leaves us passive and dependent. Perhaps resourcefulness is like a muscle: use it or lose it.

Generativity

Most of us are trained to be good implementers. Yet in today's world, you need to be someone who is a generator as well as an implementer in order to be successful in your work. But most important, you need to develop generativity in yourself so you remember that you are not helpless. You can create something out of nothing, make things happen, take on, and start things.

In summary, you can have a brilliant career strategy but still not succeed if you lack the courage to begin it, if you never listen to people (or yourself), if you give up easily on your own ideas, if you're not open to new ways of doing things, if you blame others for anything that goes wrong, if you hold rigidly to your plans even though everything points to the need to alter them, if you put on an act to impress others, if you don't keep your word, if you refuse to figure out new ways of doing things with limited resources, or if you wait for other people to tell you what to do. Developing the ten key qualities of self-development—courage, empathy, commitment, openness, responsibility, flexibility, authenticity, integrity, re-sourcefulness, and generativity—will help you win at work no mat-ter what position you have.

Richard is a good example of someone who took development of these qualities seriously and refused to be a victim. He kept going until he found what he wanted, right where he was.

Yearning for creativity

Richard had worked for a number of years for a well-known high-technology company. He held a lucrative position in the information systems department when I met him. In the past, outside of work, Richard had been very creative. He had per-formed as a musician and composed music. He had done noth-ing creative recently, though, because he was so deeply depressed about work that he lacked the energy to pursue his interests. He felt victimized, believing that he was stuck in a bor-ing job in which his creativity was not valued or appreciated.

With some encouragement, Richard began to value his artistic side once again and to feel better about himself. He decided he did not want to leave his company, but he also did not want to wait to see what would happen to him in the future. He began to take the initiative.

He explored the possibility of doing work that used more of his creative talents. He had long conversations with people in the human resource department, especially those involved in training. Together with them, he designed a new position for himself in which he leads courses in creativity.

Richard's new position has been a great match with his talents and interests. He is thrilled, and the company has retained a loyal and newly enthusiastic employee who is operating at 100 percent plus. Richard has also returned to his music in his spare time and is once again composing and performing. ●

If you're experiencing difficulties or are unhappy at work, you may think you have done something wrong. Indeed, you may have. For instance, if you consistently step on others' toes, don't keep promises, or do unacceptable work, you no doubt have created your own difficulties. But, in my experience, this is generally not the case. More likely, the problem is not what you have done but what you have *not* done. It's all the things you've thought about doing but haven't acted on, including some things you're not consciously aware of.

Take the Career Management Inventory to see how you're doing

Take the Career Management Inventory on the next four pages to find out how you are managing yourself right now.

assessment 3
career management inventory

Apply the following statements to your current job or your most recent job if you are unemployed. Be honest with yourself. Check "True" only if a statement applies at least 90 percent of the time. "N.A." means not applicable.

	True	False	N.A.
1. I am satisfied with the results I produce in my work.	___	___	___
2. I know what the "cutting edge" issues are for my field, profession, or organization.	___	___	___
3. I have recently volunteered for a new project, written a proposal, or come up with a creative new idea.	___	___	___
4. I have deliberately created a support system to ensure my success in getting where I want to go (not in staying where I am).	___	___	___
5. I belong to professional organizations and attend meetings and conferences related to my field.	___	___	___
6. My subordinates appear to be energized by their work, and I see them as competent and able.	___	___	___
7. I know where I am on the organization chart or where I am positioned in my field.	___	___	___
8. I let people around me know what I want to be acknowledged for and in what way.	___	___	___
9. I have a sponsor or mentor or a role model.	___	___	___

	True	False	N.A.
10. I have a clear direction for my career and have outlined my goals for the next three to five years.	—	—	—
11. I understand organizational structures and politics and am sensitive to them.	—	—	—
12. I know the goals and missions of my organization or of my clients' organizations.	—	—	—
13. I am fully supportive of my boss and other superiors.	—	—	—
14. I meet regularly with my supervisor to discuss my progress or have other ways in place to monitor my progress.	—	—	—
15. I seek out work or ask for work to be delegated to me.	—	—	—
16. I have told my supervisor and other relevant people about my career goals.	—	—	—
17. I ask for and take on more responsibility.	—	—	—
18. I use my imagination, ingenuity, and creativity to help solve organizational or client problems.	—	—	—
19. I take the initiative and work hard.	—	—	—
20. I follow through on projects and complete them.	—	—	—
21. I meet deadlines.	—	—	—
22. I am on time for work and meetings.	—	—	—
23. My work space (including my filing system) is functional and supports getting my work done.	—	—	—

continued

	True	False	N.A.

24. I complete communications with people I work with, particularly when I experience problems with them. ___ ___ ___

25. I keep up on my correspondence. ___ ___ ___

26. I return telephone calls as soon as possible. ___ ___ ___

27. I admit it when I make mistakes. ___ ___ ___

28. I acknowledge myself for my success. ___ ___ ___

29. I take advantage of opportunities to learn and to try new things. ___ ___ ___

30. I am up to date on the newest information, equipment, and technology in my field. ___ ___ ___

31. I keep my commitments and follow through on what I say I will do. ___ ___ ___

32. I acknowledge people around me for their contributions. ___ ___ ___

33. I can truthfully say that I love the work I do. ___ ___ ___

34. In my work, I am able to express a purpose in my life beyond making a living. ___ ___ ___

35. I have recently (within the last six months) stepped out and taken a risk in my work. ___ ___ ___

36. I can verbalize my skills and accomplishments easily. ___ ___ ___

37. I have a system for keeping track of my accomplishments. ___ ___ ___

38. I have chosen the field of work I am in and the challenges present in it. ___ ___ ___

39. I regularly put myself in situations that stimulate personal and professional growth (classes, seminars, conferences, etc.). ___ ___ ___

	True	False	N.A.
40. I present my views and ideas forcefully and persuasively.	—	—	—
41. I take responsibility for ending my own boredom and getting myself out of ruts.	—	—	—
42. I delegate tasks enough that I am freed up to do projects that interest me.	—	—	—
43. I have people who coach me on achieving my goals.	—	—	—
44. I have a balance of play and work in my life.	—	—	—
45. I give back to my community (city, neighborhood, etc.).	—	—	—
46. My people skills are as good as my technical skills.	—	—	—
47. I pay attention to my appearance, take it seriously, and view it as part of my career strategy.	—	—	—
48. My appearance reflects a positive self-image.	—	—	—
49. My appearance reflects my goals and the image I want.	—	—	—
50. I often get positive feedback about my appearance.	—	—	—
51. I follow a routine for skin care, hair care, and nail care.	—	—	—
52. Co-workers would agree that my wardrobe is current, updated, and appropriate for my work environment.	—	—	—
53. My appearance supports my efforts to market myself.	—	—	—
54. My appearance encourages people to take me seriously.	—	—	—

continued

	True	False	N.A.
55. My glasses are updated and attractive or I wear contact lenses.	___	___	___
56. My teeth are in good condition.	___	___	___
57. I am at my goal weight, healthy, and physically able to carry out my goals.	___	___	___
58. I exercise vigorously at least three times a week.	___	___	___
59. My appearance makes me look approachable.	___	___	___

60. In summary, I am currently operating at _____percent (0–100 percent plus) in

my career.

What is your score?

50–59 True: You're doing a great job of managing yourself. Clearly you are action oriented and exercising your personal power.

30–49 True: You're on the right track. Take action steps to move more statements into the True column. Take more responsibility and look less to others for blame or direction.

O–29 True: You're waiting for other people to take care of you and are in a position to be victimized. Wake up! Take steps immediately to reclaim your personal power.

What did you learn about yourself by taking the inventory? Did lightbulbs switch on? If you are not satisfied with where you are right now, is it clear to you why this is so? Did you bristle at the questions about your appearance and think appearance should have little to do with your progress, even though you have heard that first impressions are very important and are hard to change? Did it become obvious that you have taken little time to think about and plan for the future? Or did most of the items you marked "False" reveal a pattern of poor relationships, either with your boss or with your co-workers? Or is the underlying problem the fact that you are not taking good care of yourself? What patterns showed up?

Use what you have learned about yourself to create a powerful strategy for the future. Work on moving the check marks in the "False" column to the "True" column. The actions you take will enable you to stop being a victim and will alter your relationship to work.

Now go back to the inventory. What are three items you marked "False" that you would like to move toward "True"? For each of these items, write down one action you are willing to take right away.

1. _____

   _____

2. _____

   _____

3. _____

   _____

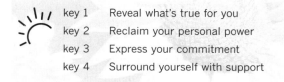

key 1   Reveal what's true for you
key 2   Reclaim your personal power
key 3   Express your commitment
key 4   Surround yourself with support

Questions to ask yourself

- Have I given all I can to succeed in my current work situation?

- If I could have it any way I wanted in my present situation, how would it be?

- What personal qualities do I need to work on developing?

Action steps to take

- Choose one personal quality you know you need to improve. Come up with a plan for working on it, and then take the first step. Some ideas: read books, take a course, participate in a personal growth workshop, meet with a counselor, hire a coach, ask a friend to help you.

- Interview two people in your company who are doing work that interests you. Get to know them. Find out what they are working on, what they think is needed in the job, what their background is, and how they landed that work.

- Raise the integrity level in your work. Be on time, meet deadlines, keep appointments, finish assignments, keep your promises. If you're a manager, keep your word with your employees, just as you do with your customers (this includes keeping appointments and doing performance reviews when you say you will). If you have trouble remembering your promises, write them down.

My company is not only not with it, it's rushing headlong into the seventeenth century.

—a client with a well-known company
   who prefers to remain anonymous

chapter 7
create a healthy work environment

The number one complaint about work I hear from my clients is that they feel unacknowledged and unappreciated for their contributions. It leaves them feeling angry and resentful, wanting to leave.

In case you think my clients are unusually whiney, let me tell you about a study conducted by a major company that was losing many talented employees it wanted to keep. The company hired independent researchers to interview former employees and discover their real reasons for leaving. More than 60 percent of those who had left cited their relationship with their manager as the major reason, noting that they did not feel appreciated or recognized for their efforts.

Over the years, I have given speeches to thousands of people. Whenever I talk about the problem of feeling unappreciated, if bosses are not in the room, people in the audience nod their heads in agreement. It is a chronic and widespread problem in the work-place. Many managers act like the drill sergeants my brother had in the Marine Corps, who said, "If you don't hear from us, you're doing great." This approach may work in the military, but it definitely doesn't work in business. It is inappropriate and shortsighted. Every time we take all the credit for a project and fail to acknowledge everyone else who contributed his or her efforts, we miss an extra-ordinary opportunity.

Like flowers and plants, people need to be cared for and nur-tured. If they are, they will blossom; if they aren't, they will wither and die. We don't get mad at flowers when they die because we haven't watered them. Why do we get mad at people who fail when we have given them little or no support or acknowledgment? We need to create a culture of acknowledgment within our companies, not just hold events once or twice a year. When I consult with com-panies, I often encourage employees to use their staff meetings to acknowledge each other regularly. Even the most cynical and hard-ened of them enjoy doing this once they get started, and find that it makes a difference.

Stop waiting for someone else to make it better

If you expect acknowledgment from your manager and are consis-tently disappointed, don't take it personally. It is likely that he or she never acknowledges anyone, ever. Acknowledgment is a weak mus-cle for many managers. Give up hoping for it and get into action by acknowledging yourself.

Keep a record of the qualities and accomplishments you are proud of, even the smallest ones. Often it's the unnoticed little things that create resentment. Pay as much attention to the way you did something as to what you did. Only you know how much courage it took for you to pick up the telephone and call a particular person, the care with which you finished a project, or the generosity involved in an action.

An appointment book is a great place to record your accomplishments. Write them down at the end of each day or week. Just two or three things that you feel really good about are enough; you don't necessarily need a long list. The important thing is to let in a feeling of pride and pleasure when you do it. Another place to record accomplishments is on the back of your pay envelope or electronic check deposit notice.

File these records of accomplishment. Or create an accomplishments folder and regularly fill it with material or brief descriptions. You will then have a history of your accomplishments that you can use to back up requests for more responsibility, a raise, or a promotion, or to review when you need to lift your spirits. Too often, we race on to the next thing and tend to forget or invalidate what we have just done. We rarely stop and take time to celebrate. If you take responsibility for filling yourself up, you will eliminate a potential breeding ground for resentment.

Of course, the next question is, what are you doing to acknowledge the people around you? Companies can be such wastelands, with everyone waiting to be acknowledged. It's like a standoff at O.K. Corral. Why don't you be the one to start? Begin with people who have the behind-the-scenes jobs and are rarely noticed: doormen, housekeepers, waiters and waitresses, carhops, gardeners, nurse's aides, cooks, videographers, editors, secretaries, file clerks, and so on. Notice what they are contributing and also how they bring themselves to their work—for example, their caring, excellence, and creativity. When we are acknowledged for the qualities we bring to an endeavor, we feel deeply appreciated and understood. This is something you can do immediately to begin to improve your working environment.

It's really okay to express appreciation to your boss too. Almost everyone who is not politically ambitious forgets to do this. You would be surprised to hear how much bosses need positive feedback, and the degree to which they appreciate it when it is sincere. Because acknowledgment is such a significant missing element in most people's work lives, one of my clients created a business addressing it. He began as a traditional image consultant, helping people increase their self-esteem. But as the years progressed, his work changed. He began to see that the real issue underlying low self-esteem was lack of acknowledgment. He now focuses on helping people acknowledge themselves and expand their ability to receive acknowledgment from everything and everyone around them. His clients have experienced dramatic increases in self-esteem, and his business has grown solely by word of mouth. His clients come from all walks of life and, surprisingly, are people who by anyone's standards are already very successful. Take a look at Chart 3 to find other approaches to creating a healthy work environment.

chart 3
nine ways to put spirit back into your work

1. Do work you love.
2. Get back on track.
3. Don't gossip and complain.
4. Learn to appreciate straight talk.
5. Become an astute observer of yourself and others.
6. Take charge of your own growth.
7. Do something about your office.
8. Get a life!
9. Take some risks.

Nine ways to put spirit back into your work

A healthy work environment is one that has spirit, unlike that of a certain company I used to consult with. I was always tempted to ask "Who died?" when I walked into its hushed offices. The following are nine things you can do to make sure you are alive at work and not contributing to a repressive atmosphere.

Do work you love

Identify the work you really want to do in your company and go after it. Make requests, volunteer, find out what it would take, create a project, form a team. Just do the work that lights you up, and then, if possible, give away, delegate, or scrap the work that is tedious or boring. Here's what Carlos did to begin creating work he loved.

Creating an internship

Carlos worked in the distribution center of a manufacturing company. He began with an entry-level job. After five years in his department, he had learned all the jobs around him. He was bored and restless when he came to see me.

Through exercises, Carlos determined that he wanted to learn to use CAD/CAM software. Having this skill would open up interesting new work and future growth opportunities. When he discovered that his background and education did not qualify him for a job in this area, he visited the CAD/CAM department and talked the manager into letting him spend some time in the department after working hours to observe and learn.

Gradually, he got permission to ask several employees to teach him. Now he spends several hours in the department each day after work. He will be positioned well when a new job opens up. To make sure he will be qualified, he also plans to take classes. Carlos is not waiting and hoping. He is already doing the work he loves and creating his own future. ●

Get back on track

These are times when work environments are confusing and unsettling. It's easy to lose sight of personal principles and goals. When everything around you is changing wildly, it's easy to get derailed. But at times like this, it's more important than ever to be grounded in who you are and what you believe in. Matt's story illustrates how to do it.

Giving 100 percent

When Matt came to see me, he was feeling depressed about his job in the cargo division of an airline company and thinking that maybe he should leave. A lot had happened in the previous two years. The company had lost ground in the market and had reorganized, resulting in a large-scale layoff. Matt, one of the few who survived the downsizing, was left with a skeleton crew. It had been depressing and scary.

Matt reported that the company was healthier now and that the outlook for the future was better but far from clear. One possibility was that his whole operation might be shut down in a year or so. As Matt talked, it became clear that he had put himself "on hold" about a year before and had been operating at about 50 percent ever since. He was not happy with himself.

Matt realized that it was a matter of personal integrity for him to give 100 percent effort in his work. We both agreed that in doing this he couldn't lose, no matter what happened to the company. He decided to pursue some good ideas he had been holding back on and to initiate some new business he had been thinking would be good for the company.

Matt decided that as long as he was with the company, he would give it his all. If the company didn't make it, he would find other work. In either case, he'd be in great shape personally, and that was what counted. His mood and productivity both rose, and he was much happier. He is on track once again. ●

It is quite likely that everyone around Matt was behaving in the same way he was when he first came to see me. Negativity is seductive. It isn't easy to step out of it, but often when you do, the people around you will, too.

Don't gossip and complain

When we are dissatisfied at work, we often act like adolescents or even younger children. For example, when we are feeling hurt, angry, or frustrated, we may enroll everyone around us in our negativity, creating a toxic environment in which everyone is busy blaming everyone else. Rarely, if ever, do we ask what responsibility *we* have in the situation or what *we* are going to do about it.

The doldrums are a way of life for the vast majority of working people. It is difficult to avoid participating in gossip and complaints, but you will never feel motivated or empowered unless you do. Many of my clients report feeling better immediately when they follow my advice to stop whining and complaining.

It is an especially common practice to complain about bosses. If you have a boss who is unethical, dishonest, alcoholic, mentally ill, sadistic, or abusive, you should definitely do something about it. But this is rarely the case. Usually, your boss is simply someone with whom you disagree, who irritates you, or who has a different style of working from yours.

Not only do we complain about bosses, but we are also expert at getting back at them: we simply withdraw our support and enthusiasm. As employees, however, it is our job to support our boss and help him or her win. When we don't, it's equivalent to walking off the field in the middle of a game. Supporting people is not the same as agreeing with them. It's a matter of continuing to be fully in the game. You know what your boss needs in order to be successful. It's hidden in your complaints: "She's so picky; she wants to see every detail." "He wants all this background material and tons of facts and figures." So give it to her or him. Stop using your energy to resist. Your relationship will immediately improve.

Not being the boss gives us the luxury to observe all the mistakes bosses make and the stupid things they do. We take on the task with relish and with little or no compassion. We forget that *bosses are us, promoted!* One day they're workers and the next day they're managers, often with no training in between.

Many of my clients have confessed that when they talk to their boss, they end their sentences with a silent "You jerk." After working with me, it gradually dawns on them that their "jerk" message is heard as clearly as if they had said it out loud. After all, we hear and respond to the music, not the words. Dropping the "jerk" message, sarcasm, or disrespect will immediately improve your relationship with your boss. You will wonder what happened to change him or her.

If you have good reason not to respect your boss and think you never will be able to do so, the question I have for you is this: Why in the world are you working for someone you don't respect? Why are you doing that to *yourself*? What does that say about *you*? If you can't respect the person you work for, leave. This is the most important relationship you have at work; it colors everything else. On the other hand, if it's just your boss's style that irritates you, tell yourself the truth about that and stop complaining.

Work always presents us with opportunities to mature in our relationships, especially if they involve authority of some kind. A great question to ask yourself when you are interacting with your boss, especially in relation to uncomfortable issues, is this: How old am I being right now? The first age that comes to you is probably correct.

In infinite adult variations, we are masterful at sulking, whining, pouting, and complaining and consider them proactive forms of communication, thinking we are making requests. Then we wonder why we don't get what we want. As soon as you take your attention off your boss and focus on the way you are conducting yourself, you will be empowered. You do know that you can't really change someone else, don't you? All you can do is change yourself. When you do that, sometimes miracles occur with other people and sometimes they don't, but you're always better off.

Learn to appreciate straight talk

One of the ways we manage to avoid feeling uncomfortable is to train the people around us not to challenge us too much. In exchange, we promise to do the same. For example, you might enroll in night school because you want to complete your degree, knowing it will help you accomplish your goals. For a while, it's easy. You even like it and settle into a routine. But then you are confronted by a cold, wintry night. You tell a friend you don't feel like going to class because of the weather, and he or she responds, "I don't blame you. I wouldn't go, either." You end up staying home, and the next time your friend doesn't want to do something, you, too, respond with "I don't blame you." That's collusion. The unspoken agreement at which you have just arrived is that if your friend doesn't push you to do things you don't want to do, you won't push him or her either, and neither of you will do "better" than the other one.

We also train our friends and family members not to give us uncomfortable feedback. As a result, we can avoid feeling bad and can manage to get our way, be left alone, or dominate other people. After a while, those around us stop trying to give us feedback because they know we will cry, bristle, laugh off or ignore what they say, argue vehemently, yell and humiliate them, or give them the silent treatment for days. They maintain their relationship with us by giving up and deciding that's just the way we are, or they stay around but withhold their affection and support. This happens at work, too. For example, there are people to whom nobody gives negative feedback because they are always defensive. And there are managers with whom no one disagrees, even when it may cost the company dearly, because he or she always humiliates people who have an opinion different from theirs.

All of us have negative behaviors. We probably developed them as defenses when we were children. They may have been appropriate at that time, but as adults we are hindered when people around us are afraid to give us feedback or think that even if they do, it will not make a difference anyway. We are skilled at our defensive behaviors and largely unaware of the effect they have on others.

I often give straightforward feedback to my clients, and even though they may find it uncomfortable, they are usually grateful and relieved. What I have to say is rarely a surprise. Usually, someone in their life has been telling them the same thing for some time, but they have been discounting it. For instance, men often say, "My wife has been telling me that for years." Whatever the "that" is, pay attention. It will cost you a lot less money to listen to your husband or wife than to hire a consultant.

Become an astute observer of yourself and others

Observing ourselves and others is a skill that is very different from analyzing or even being insightful. Often, just the act of observing other people's behavior, instead of getting caught up in it, is very powerful. It allows us to depersonalize their actions.

It is an even more powerful act to observe ourselves. This requires the ability to stand back at any given moment and observe the way we are behaving, much as if we were watching a movie in which we are the main character. Self-observation is the first step needed if we are to make changes in our lives. We need to see what we are doing before we can change it. This awareness then allows us to choose our actions. We can continue on the path we are already on, or we can alter it. If we are not observant, we are merely reacting automatically to everything around us.

Focusing on changing ourselves is much more effective than trying to change other people. It is also personally empowering. Sometimes when we change, others do, too, but that should never be our goal. If you are unhappy with the politics and climate of the company you work for, as is the case for many of my clients, of course you should do everything you can to create change. But if you do not have a group of people committed to the same goal, it may be a hopeless task. In the meantime, focus on the personal changes you can make in order to maintain your dignity and thrive in your current work environment for as long as you stay, as Annette did.

The glass ceiling

When I met Annette, she had been working for an oil company for more than thirteen years. She had been director of marketing for a number of years and had fulfilled that role very successfully. As a result, she was promoted. Initially, she was very happy about the promotion, but over time she became increasingly dissatisfied. Like most companies in this industry, her firm is dominated by men at the top levels of management. The environment is male oriented and uses left-brain skills, often to the exclusion of the right-brain skills that made Annette successful. Additionally, Annette complained that her new job has no clear definition, no power, no clear territory, and few parameters. It's all up to her to define.

Annette reported that she was acutely aware of the ways in which she was treated differently from the men around her. She knew that she was "adored" by many of these men, but she often didn't feel respected by them. She also knew that the top executives valued her; they invested in her by sending her to a premier three-month executive development program. But she had also had many experiences of not being listened to, especially in meetings. Even though she had been told that she was being groomed for an even higher position, she was often excluded from participating in important committees. Moreover, she was frequently asked to do tasks (such as proofreading manuscripts) that she knew men at her level would never be asked to do.

Annette had a lot of reasons to be angry and upset about her work environment. It was not a particularly friendly one for people with right-brain strengths, and particularly for women, but she was not interested in leaving. She was fiercely loyal to the company and extremely well paid, so it was not easy to consider moving on. And she was challenged by the difficulties she was experiencing. Most of all, she saw an opportunity for personal growth. Annette decided to focus on changing herself rather than the men around her. She began to observe herself in interactions with them.

She noticed that she did not step forward with ideas as strongly as she could. She backed down when she was challenged. She sometimes felt like a little girl, and she did not assume that she could do things without permission. She had not carved out a special niche for herself and had not acted as if she had authority. Instead, she was waiting for someone to give it to her.

Annette decided to use this challenging environment as a stimulus to stretch and grow. She committed to take actions until she was told to stop. She plans to stay with her job until it is no longer meaningful to her personally. Then, if she sees no further possibilities for personal growth, she will leave. •

Take charge of your own growth

I have noticed that a great many people who attend personal growth workshops (including mine) pay the fees themselves, even though their companies often reap the rewards of more committed, productive, and satisfied employees. Paying their own way gives them a sense of freedom to talk about whatever they wish in the workshops. If you are waiting for your company to send you to some training session or have been told there is no money for training, pay for it yourself. Do this regardless of whether it is personal growth training or technical training to update your skills and keep you current in the job market. You will feel recharged and will no longer feel victimized because you are investing in your future and taking action.

Do something about your office

Look around you. Are you inspired by what you see? Most offices are drab and cluttered, reflecting a lack of conscious awareness. Is there something about color and beauty that diminishes productivity? I think not. It's probably the opposite. I know that many companies set limits on office decor, but such parameters are similar to dress codes—there's probably a lot more latitude than you are acknowledging. Everywhere, employees are being asked to be more creative, and yet there is nothing stimulating in our work environments. So go ahead and experiment. Move things around. Try some new things. Add some beauty. Clean up the mess. Most important of all, make room for the future by clearing out the past.

Get a life!

There are two keys to having a life outside of work: learn to say no, and don't use work as an excuse. It's not healthy to have nothing but your work. The problem with an unbalanced life is that work takes on too much importance. You lose your perspective. Lighten up and remember that there is a whole world outside of your job. Time away from work usually contributes to productivity and creativity rather than detracting from it.

I know this one well. When I first started my business, I was too excited and too scared to take any time off. For almost two years,

I worked night and day, seven days a week. Then I began to have strange "attacks" during which I felt as if I were going to faint. I went to medical doctors, sure that it was a serious illness. Every one of them told me I was having a stress reaction. I told them that was impossible because I was teaching stress management seminars!

It took a visit to a therapist to uncover the fears and the behaviors that were contributing to the attacks (too much work, no play, and a combination of alcohol, caffeine, and sugar). When I stopped drinking alcohol entirely in 1981, it helped, but I replaced this addiction with another one, work. It took getting married to make a difference, but even then, at first I had to remind myself to quit work and go home. It has taken me a long time to learn to slow down, relax, and enjoy time off, to trust that all will be fine. I have even discovered that everything is better when I take time to rest and play. Perhaps you think I can do this only because I have my own business, but Laura did a great job in expanding her life outside of work, too.

A return to theater and life

Laura was feeling disenchanted with her job and ready to leave it when she attended my workshop. She had spent eight years working for a company that she described as progressive and interesting, having been there almost since its inception. She was loyal to the company and preferred to stay, but she thought her only option was to leave because she was feeling "on empty" emotionally, did not think she was taken seriously as a manager, and was having difficulty with her boss.

Laura worked hard to understand what had gone wrong with a job she used to love. She focused on herself, not the company, and took an honest look at herself. I suggested that she start with her physical appearance. She admitted that she still looked like a hippie and updated her appearance to generate more respect for herself as a leader. When we explored her relationship with her boss, I pointed out that she repeatedly backed down when presenting ideas to him. She described her boss as pragmatic, someone who valued arguing about ideas. She described herself as emotional and realized she had personalized his behavior, thinking he was disapproving of her every time he challenged her ideas. Laura began to stand up *for* her ideas, not *against* her boss.

Finally, Laura took steps to open up her life outside of work. For many years, all she had done was go to work and return home. She had stopped doing two things that served as creative and fun outlets—acting in the theater and singing. Laura put both of these activities back into her life.

Everything improved at work as a result of the changes Laura made in herself. She became a leader, and her relationship with her boss improved. She got more of what she wanted, her life was fuller, she had new creative outlets outside of work, and she no longer felt it was necessary to leave her company. ●

Take some risks

Most of us feel dead at work when we have stopped stretching and growing. Taking risks is one way to feel alive. Risks can take many forms. Margaret took a risk at work by telling the truth, and it paid off for her in a big way.

Margaret speaks out

Years ago, I attended a leadership seminar that I have never forgotten because of Margaret. One evening, we were all reporting on the homework we had done between sessions, and Margaret shared the following story. She had been working for a large, well-known service company for twenty years and had been looking forward to retiring soon. Since she had last seen us, the president of her company had called an emergency meeting of senior employees, including her, to talk about some bad publicity the company had received. In response to the question "What should we do about it?" people were making suggestions such as "We should mount a countercampaign" and "We should let the public know all the good stuff we do." Margaret told the seminar participants that she had listened for a while and then, to her surprise, found her hand snaking up and heard her own voice saying, "But, I agree with them" (meaning the critics).

The room became very quiet. The company's president, however, was very interested. As it turned out, Margaret's comment turned the whole meeting around. Perhaps the most interesting part of the story is that Margaret no longer talked about retiring. She was having too much fun. The president had created a new project for her as a result of her speaking out, and soon she was traveling all over the country to learn what had caused those negative reports and figure out what could be done to improve the company, not its publicity. ●

You are more in control of your environment than you believe yourself to be. There are things you can do to make it healthier. Do those things now.

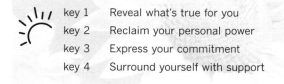

key 1   Reveal what's true for you
key 2   Reclaim your personal power
key 3   Express your commitment
key 4   Surround yourself with support

Questions to ask yourself

- Am I acknowledging the people around me for their contributions? Whom do I want to acknowledge, and for what accomplishment or special quality?

- What am I doing this year to enhance my personal or professional growth?

- Is my life well rounded and full outside of work?

Action steps to take

- Practice receiving straightforward feedback graciously—take a deep breath and say "Thank you." Don't defend yourself or argue; just ask for examples. Get feedback first from people you know and trust. If three people give you the same criticism, pay attention to it and work on changing your behavior.

- Change your office. Move things around. Take down old things on the wall and put up new things. Make it an inspiring place to be.

- Do one thing outside of work that you have been yearning to do for a long time and that you have been complaining you don't have time to do. Just schedule it and do it. Arrange the rest of your life around it and see what happens.

- Make a list of people to acknowledge and then do it. Thank them verbally, write cards, buy flowers, give concert tickets, bring in doughnuts or pizza. Just do it. Be sure you let them know why you are doing this and what it is about them that you appreciate.

We need to look at our lives with grace-full eyes.

—a workshop participant

chapter 8
bring spirituality into your work and life

Is your company a spiritual place? If you are like most people, you probably answered this question with an emphatic "No." Yet workplaces are made up of people just like you, many of whom are hungry for the same kind of environment you are. Of course, once again, it begins with you and perhaps has more to do with a way of being than a place. To quote Matthew Fox, author of *The REinvention of Work* (HarperSanFrancisco, 1994), "spirit means life, and both life and livelihood are about living in depth, living with meaning, purpose, joy, and a sense of contributing to the greater community. A spirituality of work is about bringing life and livelihood back together again."

Begin by being grateful

Learn to be grateful. Particularly in business, we tend to look at what we haven't done rather than what we have. We are obsessed with always wanting to have more or achieve more, which leaves us in a chronic state of ingratitude.

Begin your day with prayers of thanksgiving. Gratitude provides a humble and inspiring context for the whole day. Give thanks for your work and for the health to pursue it. This is the first step toward incorporating spirituality into your work.

The most important but difficult time to remember to be grateful is when you are confronted with adversity at work: working with a mean boss, being fired, being laid off, being overlooked for a promotion, not being listened to or taken seriously. If you reframe any of these situations as opportunities to learn and search for the lessons in them, they will take on a different character. Like an alcoholic or a cancer patient who learns to be grateful for the disease because of the spiritual growth and new appreciation of life that resulted, you can find something good, a blessing, in the adversity.

The lessons we learn from adversity are very personal. For some of us, it may be learning to be patient, or compassionate, especially with ourselves. For others, it may be learning to be humble, resourceful, or trusting. Or it may mean learning how to stand up for ourselves, listen to our heart, appreciate our family and friends, or let others help us. Work presents many such opportunities for learning. Marilyn's story provides a great example.

***

Marilyn's lessons

Marilyn decided it was time to leave her company when it was once again going through a reorganization. Even though she was offered other jobs within the company, none of them was really what she wanted to do. She felt ready to make a major change in her life. Marilyn came to me to talk about a job offer she had received that involved moving to another state. She was so positive about moving that I encouraged her to do it, even though there was something in the way she described the job that made me feel uneasy.

Three months later, Marilyn called from her new workplace. The company had entered into a merger that had not gone as expected, and large layoffs had resulted. Because she was "the new kid on the block" and was having trouble with her work, Marilyn was one of the first to be let go. She was receiving plenty of help from the company—outplacement services, a very generous severance package, and a paid move back—but she was upset and wanted to work on understanding what had happened.

As we talked, Marilyn recognized that she had ignored red flags during the initial interviews. She had heard rumors that her prospective boss did not like to spend time developing people, but she had dismissed them as exaggerations.

However, shortly after she arrived, Marilyn realized she needed her boss's help in adjusting to her new situation. When she requested it, he was abrupt and short with her. She withdrew and didn't ask anyone else for help. That was the beginning of a downward spiral.

Marilyn also acknowledged that she had known a merger was imminent when she took the job, which was a risky move. But what she needed to do now was stop blaming herself and just acknowledge that she had taken a risk that did not work out—period, end of story.

Finally, Marilyn revealed that she had latched onto this job, instead of exploring more opportunities, because she wanted to get away from some relationship problems at home. Her ambivalence about the move showed up in the fact that she had never sold her condominium or even disconnected her telephone. The perfection in her being forced to return and handle her problematic relationships was now apparent to her.

In the meantime, her three months away had been wonderful. She had learned a lot and had grown personally, and she now felt much stronger emotionally. She had even visited an estranged sister and healed her relationship with her.

All in all, Marilyn turned a potentially traumatic occurrence into a great opportunity for lessons: trust your intuition; even a failure is not bad; continue to ask for help when you need it; problems cannot be avoided; relationships can heal; adversity can lead to blessings. ●

Bringing spirituality into our work includes being grateful and more. It also includes the following:

- Being alive at work
- Fully expressing our uniqueness
- Trusting our intuition
- Being authentic
- Making choices from love, not fear
- Openly expressing our enthusiasm
- Laughing a lot (at ourselves and at life in general, not at others)
- Tapping our creativity for solutions
- Expressing openly our affection and caring for others

Think of your spiritual development as a muscle. How can you strengthen it? When do you feel spiritually connected? When I asked my clients these questions during a leadership workshop, the following five answers came up again and again:

When I am immersed in nature. We can get in touch with nature by, for example, hiking, climbing, camping, skiing, walking, driving in beautiful country, or working in a garden. I remember a vacation I took in Colorado with a number of families. One evening, the father of an eleven-year-old girl said to his daughter that he hadn't seen her all day and wondered whom she had been skiing with and where. She answered shyly, "I was alone. I feel closer to God when I ski alone." Those of us who live in cities, surrounded by concrete, have an even greater need for time in the country or wilderness.

When I am involved with art or music. It doesn't matter whether we are creators of art or music, or just spectators or listeners. We are awed and inspired and lose ourselves. We enter into another world.

When I am creating something. Whether we are painting, writing, finding a new way to put things together, coming up with ideas, or working with our hands, we experience the act of creating as a mysterious process that brings us closer to our Creator.

When I am doing work (paid or volunteer) that has deep meaning for me. When we are helping someone else or are fully engaged in a project we believe in, we leave our egocentric concerns behind and feel the joy of committing to something bigger than ourselves.

When I am quiet inside. Praying, meditating, chanting, or reading books of a spiritual nature can lead us to feel connected to something outside ourselves, some greater source of energy and strength.

As you will see in the following story, Pamela is someone who put spirituality into her work and life by choosing work that had meaning for her.

Full circle

Pamela began her career as a social worker. After earning her master's degree, she worked for many years with nonprofit organizations. Then she felt the urge to make a change and explore the business world. She ended up at a large and rapidly growing market research company. She worked in a variety of roles there, largely in the human resource area, taking on increasingly demanding assignments.

After five years with the company, Pamela came to see me. She declared that she was hungry for work with a "passionate purpose." Wisely, she decided to quit her job and take some time off before beginning a job search—"One of the best things I've done," she later told me.

As a result of exercises, conversations, and reflection, Pamela decided to return to the world of nonprofit organizations and explore a leadership role. She identified three areas of interest and began networking. After accepting a job as assistant director of a community organization, she reported that she was thrilled to be earning enough to live comfortably (although less than before), to have a job in which she could make a difference in people's lives, to be learning about fundraising and budgeting, and to be bringing her business experience to the nonprofit world. It was like closing a circle, and it felt very satisfying for to her. ●

chart 4

sixteen ways to incorporate spiritual practices into everyday life

1. Simplify your life.
2. Decide what is "enough."
3. Be creative.
4. Contribute to other people.
5. Be present to the grandeur of nature.
6. Respect your body.
7. Look with "grace-full" eyes.
8. Pray, chant, or meditate.
9. Read inspiring literature or listen to inspiring tapes.
10. Participate in areas of continued growth and development.
11. Make choices and take actions from your heart.
12. Listen to or play music, sing, or dance.
13. Act with integrity.
14. Write in a journal regularly.
15. Have fun everywhere (including at work!).
16. Spend time with people you love.

Incorporate spiritual practices into everyday life

The following are sixteen practices my clients came up with that may help you deepen your spiritual connection and bring spirituality into your work and life.

Simplify your life

Like most people today, you are probably hungrier for more time than you are for more money. Simplifying your life will reduce clutter and complications. It will allow you to be more present in each day and each moment and create more quiet time.

Decide what is "enough"

You can decide for yourself what is enough, both financially and materially, and then choose to be happy with that. You do not have to be led by the dictates of a consumer-driven society. Living by the principle that happiness is not getting what you want but wanting what you have will enable you to reduce the constant urge to produce and earn more. You will have peace of mind. Cure yourself of affluenza, a dis-ease of the soul characterized by a constant state of envy and desire for more than you have.

Be creative

Paint, draw, write, build a car from scratch, sculpt, sew, knit, weave, cook, carve wood, renovate a house or restore furniture, design a computer. Any form of creating can give you access to exploring the unknown, the mysterious. You don't have to be good, just engaged. Don't forget to use your creative gifts at work. Dan is an example of someone who combined creativity and business.

Web pages

Dan worked in the claims department of an insurance company. He was competent technically and a loyal employee. When we first talked, he had been working at his company for twenty years. He was angry and frustrated because he had been overlooked for promotion several times. He felt unappreciated and found his work unsatisfying because it lacked opportunities for creativity.

Dan began his journey toward being a happy employee again by exploring different avenues outside of work because he saw no possibilities to do so at his job. First, he applied for different but related jobs at other companies, but none of them appealed to him. Then he tried operating a business on the side and took painting and writing classes. None of these was "it," either.

Then, again on his own time, Dan began to explore the Internet and the World Wide Web. He discovered that he loved designing Web pages and that his attention to detail, combined with his creativity, produced great results. Dan talked to his boss, describing his newfound ability and the need he saw for his company to have a Web site. After a while his boss gave him the green light, and Web page design and maintenance turned into full-time work.

Even though Dan was much happier at work, he casually applied for a job with a small but growing high-technology company. He was surprised and thrilled when he was hired to create Web pages for its customers. He received a big raise, and his new company is very appreciative of his creative talents. Dan feels "in synch" now, peaceful, and grateful. ●

Contribute to other people

Whenever we create intimacy or oneness with others or actively express our love or appreciation, we feel filled up and part of something bigger than ourselves. In every interaction with people, there is an opportunity to contribute. It takes awareness and being present. Even receiving is a form of giving. Learning to listen to other people's concerns and ideas and to respect their ways of doing things is one of the greatest gifts you can give.

Be present to the grandeur of nature

The rhythms and cycles of nature are a reminder that it is natural to have up and down times, periods of both high and low productivity. Immerse yourself in the beauty of nature to be reminded of how insignificant your concerns are in the grand scheme of things.

Respect your body

When you exercise regularly, choose healthy foods to eat, and say no to alcohol, tobacco, and drugs, you are treating your body like a temple. If you learn to practice yoga, tai chi chuan, or other Eastern forms of movement, you will feel in touch with a sense of unity or wholeness. When you dance with joy or move your body in play, you are using yourself more fully than when you just use your mind. You feel more balanced. Your body carries its own wisdom and will give you important messages if you learn to listen.

Look with "grace-full" eyes

It is empowering and inspiring to focus on the fullness and blessings in your life. Open your eyes and appreciate your family, your health, your challenging and growth-inspiring experiences, the love that surrounds you, the down times, nature, the fact that you have food, hot water, electricity, clothes, and money enough for what you need. The list goes on and on. When you are filled with gratitude, awe, and reverence for your life, your complaints become truly petty and insignificant. When you adopt an "attitude of gratitude" and appreciate the miracles around you, gratitude serves as the foundation of your life, regardless of your circumstances.

Pray, chant, or meditate

Practices such as prayer, chanting, and meditation quiet your body and mind. They allow you to plug into a higher source of energy and inspiration, get grounded, let go, and be guided by your intuition. Some people have even started prayer groups at work.

Read inspiring literature or listen to inspiring tapes

Reading inspiring books and articles, poetry, or great literature or listening to inspiring tapes will return you to hope and optimism. These resources will rekindle your spirit and revitalize you. They will connect you to other people who are also confronted by the same challenges you are and will help you feel more in touch with the human community.

Participate in areas of continued growth and development

Take courses, workshops, and seminars in areas that stretch you and help you continue to learn new things throughout your lifetime. Doing so will keep your spirit alive and remind you of the joy of growth, even when it is painful. Many people report that personal growth workshops have been spiritual experiences for them.

Make choices and take actions from your heart

Some decisions you make will seem to defy logic or rationality, but you will know they are the right choices if they come from your heart as well as your mind. Have the courage to listen to your heart and act on its wisdom.

Listen to or play music, sing, or dance

Music and movement will open up your heart and spirit in a way that conversation cannot. You gain access to something different when you sing or dance. You feel on a nonverbal, often deeper, level. You open up creativity.

Act with integrity

Rid your life of abuse. Leave any situation you believe is abusive or stand up to the bullies in your life. Make sure your integrity is expressed in all areas of your work and life. Often, your health will serve as a barometer, letting you know whether you are on track or something is wrong. Complete your communications with people and come to terms with events and things, and then let go of the past.

Write in a journal regularly

When you put your thoughts on paper, you will more easily find the silence inside. Writing not only clarifies things but also replenishes the soul and opens up creativity. It can be a form of meditation.

Have fun everywhere (including at work!)

Fun is an expression of your spirit. When you are playful, you spark playfulness in others, too. Lighten up. Remind yourself that you are, as one personal growth workshop leader put it, "just an interruption in the long life of cockroaches."

Spend time with people you love

You will experience your capacity for love and your connection to a higher power when you are in the presence of love and are expressing it.

Even though you may find that many of these practices can be accomplished only outside of work hours, the results will spill over into your work. If you examine your life right now, you will probably see that you talk, think, or read about these practices more than you actually do them. Doing them as a discipline will make the difference. Just start with one.

If you are wrestling with the question of whether it is possible to be empowered where you work now or whether you need to leave, read on. Part III offers help in making a good decision and in applying the four keys to leaving if you decide to go.

key 1	Reveal what's true for you
key 2	Reclaim your personal power
key 3	Express your commitment
key 4	Surround yourself with support

Questions to ask yourself

- How do I define spirituality?

- When do I feel most spiritual? At these times, where am I and what am I doing?

- How can I bring more spirituality into my work and life?

Action steps to take

- Go back to Chart 4 in this chapter and circle one spiritual practice you want to incorporate into your life. Then do it.

- Open up a conversation with someone at work about spirituality—how that person views it and nurtures it and how he or she incorporates it into work.

- Start a recycling program at your company or some other project that honors the earth and its resources. Alternatively, find a community project for the company to support that requires the efforts of employees, not just money, such as Habitat for Humanity. Or investigate ways in which your company could be more socially responsible in the way it conducts business. If you don't do something about it, who will?

part three

if you decide to leave

Sometimes you have to stop the world and get off to really change your life.

—a member of my writing support group

chapter 9

did you give it everything you've got first?

Your relationship with work is a lot like any other relationship that has meaning in your life. The only way you are going to feel good about severing that relationship is if you know you gave it your best effort. Then, if you decide to leave, you can go with peace of mind, knowing you did everything you could to make it work while you were there.

Five things to do before you decide to leave

Perhaps you have concluded that for you, the scales are decidedly tipped toward leaving. Even in this case, give it all you've got before you make a final decision. Make sure you're not being a victim and that you've done everything you can to make it work where you are. Here are five things to do before making your decision.

chart 5
five things to do before you decide to leave

1. Fully explore options where you are.
2. Have the courage to say no.
3. Stay long enough to win the prize.
4. Take on something new at work that energizes you.
5. Take a sabbatical.

Fully explore options where you are

Ask for what you really want. If the job you want doesn't exist, create a new position on the basis of what's wanted, needed, and missing and what matches your gifts. If part-time work might be the answer, or working from home one day a week, ask for it. Don't leave before asking.

Have the courage to say no

If you are swamped with work and feel "burned out," have the courage to say no when asked to take on something else. Other people can't know all you are doing and will continue to give you work until you say "Stop." If you are single, ask yourself whether the long hours are truly justified or are a way to avoid confronting empty time alone. Schedule activities after work, such as that class you have always wanted to take. Pay for it. Then, when someone asks you to do some extra work, look at your calendar and say, "Sorry, I can't. I'm booked." Don't discuss your other plans because they might sound unimportant to you at the moment and you might go back on your promise to yourself. Support your intention to have a life of your own outside of work.

Stay long enough to win the prize

Many people leave their job in frustration before the rewards come in; then they end up feeling unsuccessful. We live in a society addicted to speed and instant solutions and have forgotten that it takes time for many things to happen. I have worked with many people who quit jobs after one or two years and left with the feeling that they hadn't accomplished anything. Give yourself long enough.

Take on something new at work that energizes you

We all fall into a rut and become bored after a while, especially if we have been working for many years at the same job. We all need new projects, new relationships, new challenges to keep us energized and growing. It's up to us to seek them out.

Take a sabbatical

Leaving can take many different forms. Maybe you just need a complete break from work that is longer than a vacation to pursue some different interests or simply to do nothing. Why not request either a paid sabbatical or some time off with no pay?

I'm a veteran of sabbaticals. I have taken one myself, and as a career coach I have walked many clients through them. Having experienced firsthand their powerful benefits, I am convinced that everyone should take sabbaticals at regular intervals.

Your initial reaction to this idea may be that other people can do it, but it's impossible for you. You may be thinking "I can't afford it," "My boss wouldn't let me go," "My company has never done it before," "Things would fall apart if I left," or "They'd never agree to it." You may be right, but you will never know until you ask, and you may be pleasantly surprised, like Sam was.

The classics

Sam is a principal in a successful management consulting firm. He is respected at the national level for his work. He also writes poetry and is passionate about the classics, history, and philosophy. When Sam attended my career workshop, he identified a desire to write and then began writing poetry occasionally, even taking a class in it. But inevitably, writing was put on a back burner as Sam became consumed with his consulting work. He enjoyed his clients and co-workers, and his compensation escalated as his reputation spread. Yet every time we met, he expressed an unfulfilled yearning to study the classics and write.

Years later, after lots of coaching from friends and me, Sam began writing poetry again, this time everywhere he went—in coffee shops, on airplanes, at every opportunity—and he mustered the courage to make a highly unusual request of his firm. He asked for a three-week break from work that summer to attend a renowned literature course offered at a famous college in the Northeast. The answer, surprisingly, was yes.

Sam was in heaven during those three weeks and discovered what he felt to be his "calling." And amazingly, his practice soared when he was gone. When Sam got out of the way, his team members took over and proved their worth. Sam has since negotiated a study sabbatical every summer and is gone for six weeks at a time now. He has also been surprised to discover that his clients love talking to him about his studies. He always includes his studies on his résumé now and believes they have enriched his life in immeasurable ways. ●

When I decided to take a sabbatical, I had grave doubts at first. Would my business fall apart? What would happen to my clients?

What would I do with myself without goals or agendas? Isn't it indulgent, irresponsible? What would people say? Perhaps not surprisingly, all these concerns and objections dissolved once I made the decision to do it. They will for you, too.

I used to think that only college professors and people with lots of money could take sabbaticals. I now know that where you work and how much money you make are important, but commitment is the decisive factor. Once you make the commitment, you'll figure out *how* to do it. You will discover a resourcefulness you didn't know you had, especially in regard to money. As one of my clients said in the third month of her sabbatical, "Every time I review my budget, I find one more month I can take." You may decide that it is worthwhile to scale down your lifestyle for a while, use the savings you have been accumulating for emergencies or special events (isn't this one?), sell some stocks, or borrow money, knowing you will more than make up for it later.

Increasingly, businesses are responding positively to requests for sabbaticals and are beginning to see their value. Don't let the fact that it's never been done in your company or that you have lots of responsibility stop you from asking. You can take a sabbatical for any number of reasons: to rest and heal your body or your spirit; to design a more balanced work life; to stimulate your brain or replenish your soul; or to sort out what to do with your life.

I have been writing a newsletter for more than twelve years. In one issue, I wrote about a two-month sabbatical I had taken during the summer of 1994. More readers responded to that newsletter than to any prior one. Many people I talked to expressed a yearning for a break from work. They wanted time to think about things, dream, explore new areas, organize or clean up, read, write, play or rest, and spend time with family—to "cocoon," in the words of Frederic Hudson and Pamela McLean in their book *Life Launch* (Hudson Press, 1995). Let me tell you about my own sabbatical and what happened as a result.

My sabbatical

At the time I decided to declare myself on sabbatical, I knew I was tired, but I did not realize how deeply exhausted I was until I actually stopped working. In retrospect, I think I may have been "running on empty" for about a year. My fatigue was not related to lack of sleep or overwork. It was due more to internal fears, worries, and pressures stemming from the way I was running my business. Also, I had drifted far away from where my heart was in my work.

When I finally took a break, I felt as if my brain were incapable of forming a coherent thought. I found it difficult to listen. I was bored, disinterested in, and irritated by the very work I used to love. I was scared that the "fire" had gone out and would never return. I had no idea what I wanted to do in the future or where the energy to do it would come from.

So I emptied my calendar. I slept late. I went for long walks. Although I am usually gregarious, I did not want company and was alone a lot. I read books—nothing related to work, mostly mysteries. I spent time with children, neighbors, friends, and family. I didn't talk about work. I went camping. I cleaned out closets, files, and drawers. I threw out the past, discarding reams of paper. I wrote in my journal every day. With the help of a spiritual advisor, I focused on moving fear outside of me and on finding trust and peacefulness inside. I started to work with my hands, embroidering again after a twenty-year hiatus. I met with a nutrition consultant and cooked some good meals. I cried on and off with little warning and for no obvious reason.

At the end of eight weeks, I began to feel better. The fires began to burn again. I remembered what I loved about my work. New projects began to tease for definition and fulfillment at the edge of my brain.

The outcomes from my sabbatical were unexpected and extraordinary. One of them was an insight into the way I had been working—"full-tilt boogie or crash"—with nothing in between. I really hadn't known how to pace myself or how to let go in "off" times. Now I am learning to notice when I am tired. I incorporate breaks into my workday. I even take naps occasionally, and I do not drive myself as hard as I used to. I incorporate physical activities into my life more instead of being overly focused on cerebral work, as so many of us are today. I continue to meditate, pray, and write in my journal. I notice that when I do these things regularly, I am less worried and more peaceful.

I also made some decisions. When I returned to work, I moved my office into my home to simplify my life. Without the high overhead I used to have, I am now able to focus on what is really important to me in my work. Like Phoenix rising from the ashes, I experienced a burst of creativity after the sabbatical. New work was born out of this time: this book, new workshops, new projects. ●

I redesigned my work and life and ended up staying with my business, just as Sam did. You might, too. Taking this time for yourself is very important when you feel burned out. Resting and creating new work habits may allow you to stay. On the other hand, permanently leaving may be the only answer, or you may not even have the option of staying. Taking a sabbatical even during unemployment may still be the best thing you could do for yourself.

Taking a complete break is the opposite of what we usually think we should do when we are unemployed. Understandably, our main focus is to get another job as quickly as possible. But moving to something else right away can be a big mistake, and taking some time can work wonders. Here's what Sandy did.

Around the world

For eight years, Sandy had put everything she had into her work with a computer company. With great sadness, she reluctantly admitted that things had gone sour. The work climate had changed dramatically. What once had been an exciting start-up company was now a stodgy, bureaucratic business. She had loved the boss she started out with, but he had recently been fired. The person who replaced him did not appreciate or value her work.

Sandy decided it was time to go, but she had no idea what she wanted to do next and felt too angry and cynical to begin another job right away. To the amazement of her friends and family, she walked away from her very lucrative job, with no alternative plans in place. At the age of thirty-five and single, she felt free to do anything she wanted. She decided to take a six-month trip by herself to Europe and the Far East.

During our first session after her return, Sandy told me that the trip had healed her. It had restored her belief in herself and her self-confidence, and she was now able to put her past work experience into perspective. She was energized and ready to look at what was next.

Sandy is now in graduate school, working on a master's degree in human resources. She is excited about this field and is clear that her first love is working with people. She believes that her past work experiences have given her a lot to contribute. ●

Getting another job as quickly as possible is usually not the best answer. I do not agree with the common advice that the best time to get a job is when you already have one. I sometimes encourage people to leave their job and *then* look for the next one, for two reasons:

1. It is extremely difficult to manage with integrity a full-time job, a family and social life, and a job search.

2. Sometimes a work situation is so toxic that our energy is depleted and we feel negative about everything. In this case, it is better to make a clean break. Give yourself time to regain your energy, self-respect, confidence, and optimism.

If you are unemployed, you may be feeling panicky about money (even if you have lots of it). However, my experience with clients has shown that people are extremely resourceful when they need to be. My clients always come up with ways to take care of themselves. Then they shift into a relaxed mode and, surprisingly, are no longer in a hurry to work. They actually begin to enjoy the time off.

Grabbing another job right away may be jumping from the frying pan into the fire. So take time away from work to think about what you really want to do next with your life. You may decide that the best answer is school, part-time work, a series of interesting and challenging projects, a business of your own, work with an entirely different kind of company, or a complete career change. It takes time to make these decisions. You don't make them happen by rushing into the next job.

Reinvent yourself

Many people who work for large corporations are snobs about working anywhere else. It's one thing to be proud of your company; it's another to think it's the only great game in town. In my experience, people only *think* they know how it is anywhere else. Their perceptions are erroneous and colored by prejudices.

Some of my clients who work for large organizations have been amazed to discover bright, competent people working for small companies. In addition, they have discovered an excitement and a vitality that are often missing in bigger companies. Once you get used to not having some corporate perks, you will probably find it thrilling to contribute to building a company. You get to do a little bit of everything. The perks are replaced with the satisfaction of knowing that what you do really counts.

Keep an open mind to other possibilities, too, such as joining a good multilevel marketing company. Most people cringe at the thought, but don't decide against one before you have investigated it thoroughly. Some of these companies are very sophisticated, have been around a long time, have credibility in the marketplace, and could be just what you are looking for. Joining one could give you the opportunity to develop your own business, work at home, meet great people, and earn as much as you are able.

But what about all the time you spent in school to get to where you are now? Don't worry about that. It may have little to do with where your heart is in your work, how your talents can be used, or where the best fit is for you in terms of people, business, and the way work is conducted. Earning the degree is just one step in managing your career. My experience with people who have moved into new arenas is that their educational background is never entirely lost. It has often been a help to them, as Roberta's story shows.

The clue

It was Roberta's necklace that gave me the clue to where her heart really was. She requested my help after she had earned a coveted M.B.A. degree from one of the best schools in the country and had been working for a big accounting firm for several years. A recent poor performance review had impelled Roberta to seek help. She was in an acute state of suffering and confusion when we first met. She believed there must be something wrong with her.

Roberta had done all the right things and didn't know why they weren't working. It took her a long time to admit that her interest was in a different area. It took her even longer to admit that she didn't fit her own picture of a successful M.B.A. graduate and to give herself permission to explore some other kind of work.

Roberta's necklace was a major clue that led to her new future. It was striking and unusual, a creative and artistic expression, in stark contrast to the rest of her formal business attire. My asking about it uncovered a larger interest in art, travel, and entrepreneurism.

Once Roberta gave herself permission to be authentic in her work and her personal life, new possibilities opened up. She landed a marketing job with a large, successful travel business. Marketing allowed her to use her creative abilities. She loved the informal atmosphere, and she and her co-workers enjoyed each other. Roberta's education is a great asset in her new work. Her long-term goal is to open a retail store filled with art objects she collects from all over the world. The travel she will be doing in her present job is a step in that direction. ●

Roberta reinvented herself as an artistic person who was able to make use of her great business background. Most people worry that if they reinvent themselves, they will lose considerable income. Because this is such a common concern, let me tell you about Brian, who made a change and *did* lose money.

Money isn't everything

Brian was working for a large, prestigious law firm but felt as if he were dying. He was bored and was not interested in his work. He also felt unappreciated, knew he was unfairly compensated for his efforts in comparison with his co-workers, and had been overlooked for advancement. It was hard to tell which problem had come first.

When I asked Brian what he was really interested in, the answer was easy. Politics had been his passion for years; he had devoted all his spare time to working in candidates' campaigns. He had not made a move to change careers, though, because he didn't see how he could make a transition to the political arena and continue to support himself in his current lifestyle. Because of these financial concerns, Brian was not ready to leave his firm. So we first focused on making things better there.

He gave it his best shot. He met with his superiors. He made specific requests for more remuneration and more interesting work, and he worked hard. Nothing changed. He still lacked interest in his work and still felt unappreciated. When he finally decided to look for other work, he knew he had given 100 percent and was ready to leave.

When an opportunity arose for Brian to work in the legal department of a small city government nearby, he decided to take it, even though it meant a $20,000 cut in salary. He chose to make the sacrifice because he knew it would put him closer to the political scene he loved.

I talked to Brian after he had been working for six months at the new job. He reported that he was having a lot of fun being a lawyer again, was positioned well to meet people politically, and in general was having a great time. Money didn't seem to be a problem. He had been able to keep the things that meant the most to him; the only change he had made was to take on a roommate. Clearly, the loss of some money was not nearly as important as waking up in the morning eager to go to work. •

As Ralph Waldo Emerson said, "Money often costs too much." In my experience, few people lose money when they make a change in their work life that is an improvement. Most people end up earning as much or *more* when they leave jobs they dislike and move on to something they love.

Part-time work may be an answer

One last thought about changing your work situation: a part-time job may be the answer. Many people today work two to three days a week at professional jobs. There is a new receptivity to this idea, and it is working well for both employers and employees. It's true that if you take this route, you will probably be left out of meetings and some exciting assignments, but that may be a big relief because you will be free to focus on the work you like to do. On your days off, you will have precious time available to be with your children, pursue hobbies, start a business of your own, or write a novel. Just be sure to ask for enough money to cover the expenses of health insurance and days off if these are not covered by the company.

There is no one way to be successful in your work. And there is no particular value in having a business of your own, working for a large corporation, or working for a small company. The only important question is this: Where is the fit for *you* that will enable you to blossom and fully express your passions, talents, skills, and abilities? If you have tried everything and none of your efforts has made a difference, it's time to leave. Be sure to do so with dignity.

Eight steps for leaving with dignity

If you choose to leave your job or are forced out, decide that you will leave with your head held high. Begin by taking responsibility for any part of the situation you can so that you will not feel like a victim. Be sure to look for the "gift" in going. Regardless of your reason for leaving, there are ways to conduct yourself that will make a big difference in your ability to get on with your life afterward. The following eight steps will help you leave with dignity and self-respect intact.

chart 6
eight steps for leaving with dignity

1. Resolve any negative emotions.
2. Stay present in body and spirit until you actually leave.
3. If you are being laid off or fired, ask to leave as soon as possible.
4. Complete all your work if possible, especially if you are leaving voluntarily.
5. Be sure to say good-bye.
6. When colleagues ask you what happened, talk instead about what you will be doing next.
7. Ask for everything you want, even if you think the answer will be no.
8. After you leave, don't spend a lot of time talking with former co-workers.

Resolve any negative emotions

The first step in leaving well is to resolve whatever negative emotions you have so that you can be open about your most recent work experience during job interviews. You do not want to be dragged into a swirl of emotion and resentment about it. Let yourself fully feel any grief and loss related to leaving. Do this whether you were fired, were let go, or quit. If you do not take care of these feelings, they *will* surface again—in your job search, during a job interview, or on the next job.

In a job search, these emotions show up as a general cautiousness. They keep you from enthusiastically going after what you really want or even from being willing to try again in a field of work you really like. In a job interview, your efforts to repress unresolved emotions can deplete your energy, generate anxiety, or make you appear detached and disinterested.

How do you resolve these feelings? When you are alone or with people you trust, express fully all the anger you have about leaving. Decide whether you also need to communicate with the people involved, either face-to-face or through a letter. After you have written the letter, you can decide whether or not to mail it. It doesn't really matter. Often, just writing it is enough. To complete the process, be sure to forgive everyone, including yourself. The last and perhaps most important step is to look back to see what lessons you can learn from this experience.

Stay present in body and spirit until you actually leave

Keep your attention on your work and make sure you don't withdraw. If you have been fired or laid off, co-workers who are aware of the fact may feel embarrassed, guilty, and unsure of how to act with you. They will be waiting for you to give them a cue. If you begin to withdraw, they will, too; if you don't, they won't. Like it or not, it's up to you to make them feel comfortable about this.

If you are being laid off or fired, ask to leave as soon as possible

You may be concerned about "buying time" to avoid unemploy ment and think you will be all right staying for a while. But it's just kidding yourself to think you will find another job during this time. It usually doesn't happen, if for no other reason than the fact that you are too busy with the current job, or are depressed. There's really no reason for you to stay once you have been asked to go. The longer you stay, the more painful it will be for you and every-one else.

Complete all your work if possible, especially if you are leaving voluntarily

Completing projects and tying up loose ends is something you need to do as much for yourself as for the people you are leav-ing behind. Keep your integrity and pride intact in your work, and you will leave with a free mind. Leave behind documents and materials that don't belong to you, and make sure you have made it easy for those who remain. It's smart not to burn bridges. Surprisingly, past bosses can become your best allies in the new direction you carve out for yourself when you are hon-est with them throughout the whole process and handle it with integrity.

Be sure to say good-bye

If you are feeling good about leaving, as did one of my clients, who deliberately designed herself out of a job during a restructuring, give yourself a party. Most people have a hard time saying good-bye, so take responsibility for planning an event yourself if no one else does. For example, invite a few co-workers to lunch. Let them know how much you have appreciated your relationships with them. If you don't do this in a group format, be sure to do it one-on-one. Whether you are leaving voluntarily or being let go, it is really important to say good-bye to the people you care most about. Otherwise, you will have a lingering sense of incompletion. If you are being let go, request some time just to say good-bye.

When colleagues ask you what happened, talk instead about what you will be doing next

When your work associates ask about your reasons for leaving, don't rehash the injustice of being let go or how awful your job was. Once the decision has been made, it's time to focus on the future and new possibilities, even if your current plans include no more than taking some time off to decide. Talking negatively with your co-workers, clients, customers, or vendors will only fuel your anger and depression. You'll have plenty of time away from work to deal with your emotions; don't spend the little time you have left at work doing it.

If you are considering suing your company, think it through very carefully before deciding. You may be angry and hurt, even justified in your complaints, but forgiveness, not revenge, may be the release you need. People always underestimate the energy and time it takes to conduct a lawsuit. Remember that if you do proceed with a lawsuit, you will remain emotionally entangled with the past until the suit is resolved. It may not be worth it.

Ask for everything you want, even if you think the answer will be no

Before you leave, ask for the help you will need so that you will not wish you had when it is too late to do so. Avoid letting your emotions get in the way of thinking about what you will need in the months ahead. Even with firings, companies will sometimes do a lot for their employees because the failure was in large part theirs, too. Perhaps the company made a mistake in the hiring process or did not provide the support needed for you to succeed, or perhaps the company changed and the fit became wrong. Sometimes a manager knows he or she should have let an employee go a long time ago but did not have the courage to do so.

After you leave, don't spend a lot of time talking with former co-workers

Don't rehash all the injustices you suffered. It's understandable to want to talk with former co-workers, not only to stay in touch but also to get the scoop on what's happening back at the company. If you keep talking about the past, however, you will be mired in negativity, not inspired. You will just keep yourself stuck and unable to move on if you indulge in too much of this, and you won't help the people left behind, either. In conversations with former colleagues, focus on what you are doing for yourself now, what you are looking forward to, and what help you need from them, especially in terms of contacts or resources.

If you do these things, you will leave with your dignity intact and your head held high. Then your job is to take time to figure out what's next and where the fit will be perfect for you.

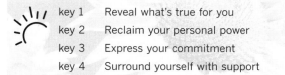

key 1   Reveal what's true for you
key 2   Reclaim your personal power
key 3   Express your commitment
key 4   Surround yourself with support

Questions to ask yourself

- Is it time for a sabbatical?

- How could I work out a sabbatical with my company? How much time do I want away from work?

- If I am leaving, am I angry, bitter, or resentful? If the answer is no, has anyone told me that I seem angry?

- Is there anything I feel incomplete about in this job? If yes, what is it? What do I need to do to gain a feeling of closure?

Action steps to take

- Pretend you could arrange a sabbatical. Plan it out. How much would it cost to do it? How could you make it work financially?

- Interview someone who has taken a sabbatical and loved it. How did this person do it? What were the rewards? How did he or she convince the company to say yes? If the person was unemployed at the time, how did he or she determine that it was the right thing to do? Was his or her family apprehensive about the decision? If so, how was this resolved?

- Interview three people who have left their jobs and are now working in very different situations and loving it. Find out what's different and why they are happier now. If you worry that you won't be able to find great people outside your present company, be sure to ask your interviewees whether they respect and like their new co-workers.

- If you are sad, angry, or hurt about leaving, talk out your feelings with a friend. Talk until you feel empty or at least much lighter. Alternatively, use a journal to work through these feelings.

- Find a good therapist and use the unhappiness and disappointment of this recent adverse work experience to move your personal growth light-years ahead.

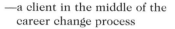

I'm discovering me—who I am—for the first time.

—a client in the middle of the
  career change process

chapter 10
if you are unemployed for a while

What if you were to consider being unemployed a gift and not a disaster? When else will you have the time to explore fully what's next? Once you are working again, you will have little time for reflecting, talking to lots of people about what they do, discovering what's happening in a particular field, finding out who the big players are, or learning about the reputations of people and companies. This is the perfect opportunity to gain an overview of a field and build a network. It may even be the time to explore something entirely new, something you have always wanted to do. And because it's only possible to spend about five hours a day looking for work anyway, you can slow down and spend some time with family and friends, or read, or just think.

Have the courage to slow down

The good thing about being unemployed is that it gives you a chance to reevaluate your priorities and values. So come up with a plan to give yourself time to reflect and explore. Overestimate how long you will need to find the right job; it usually takes longer than people think. This way, you can avoid panicking or being hard on yourself if it really does take that long.

There are several things that make it difficult to take your time. One is the widely held belief that it's indulgent and unproductive to rest or take time to think. Yet, especially if you failed at your last job, this is what you need the most.

Another thing that creates pressure to move too fast is fear about money. It doesn't matter how much money you make; everyone is scared about money. Most of us live from paycheck to paycheck. Even people who have saved a lot of money are afraid to use it for time off. We hear thundering voices in our head warning us that we may go into debt, we will not have enough for retirement, and so forth. These voices are amplified right after a job loss. But I have noticed that as the weeks go by, people relax. Their attitudes and behaviors change. Usually the fear about money starts to go away. People become resourceful and get used to living with less. They sell something, such as stocks or a second car, to bring in some money. Or they borrow from savings, scale down their lifestyle, get a part-time job, or take on projects that bring in money. What surprises me the most is that then they are no longer in a hurry to get back to work. They want to enjoy life a little and take their time about entering into another work situation. They want to be sure it's a good one for them. They have discovered that they have an ability to survive and a newfound resourcefulness. Some of them change their lives permanently as a result of this experience.

A third thing that can get in the way of taking your time is a need to feel useful. We all need to work at something. We need to have a reason to get up in the morning and a place to go where we will be missed if we don't show up. You may begin to be impatient if you don't find that right away. You may feel useless unless you are contributing somewhere. This may be the time to do some volunteer work.

Another reason you may move too quickly is pressure from other people, usually spouses who are scared or perhaps embarrassed. I knew one person (not a client) who never even told his wife and children that he was unemployed. He kept it a secret until he had another job. He just kept going to the outplacement office each day as if he were working. I think unemployment is too much of a burden for any one person to handle alone, and hiding it from one's immediate family disempowers them.

It's really important to manage yourself so that you are not panicked during your time between jobs. If you interview for a job when you are panicked, the interviewers will feel your neediness and back off. After all, they are not interested in hiring you in order to help pay your rent and buy your groceries. The biggest danger, though, is that you may ignore any "red flags" that come up in the interview process. If you do this, I guarantee they will come back to haunt you. Read Maggie's story as an example.

A hasty move

Maggie came to see me in shock and dismay after failing at a new job. She had loved her previous job as a market researcher with a focus on international companies. She speaks and reads Japanese and loves anything with an international focus. She had traveled to Japan, Indonesia, Europe, and South America and had worked on interesting projects. For several years, her work had been very challenging and satisfying. When the priorities of the firm shifted, however, the international work that Maggie enjoyed so much disappeared. All that was left was research in the United States, which required her to do a great deal of domestic travel and work extremely long hours. Maggie felt burned out and decided she had to leave her job.

When Tom, a colleague who had recently left the company to start a small research firm with a partner, heard that Maggie was ready to leave, he invited her to join them. Maggie was frightened of being unemployed, so she jumped at the offer, thinking that a new environment was what she needed. She took the job with very little thought but with high hopes, even though it, too, involved research with no international work. She had only one short interview with Tom's partner, Bob, who headed the firm. Several times during the interview, Maggie was struck by how different she was from Bob, but she dismissed the differences as unimportant, and she asked very few questions about the nature of the consulting work itself.

Six months later, Maggie was again out of work and wondering what had happened. She had failed in her new job and had been asked to leave. As she reflected on the experience, she began to see where she had missed the cues that the job was not a good fit for her. She also began to understand the importance of her relationship with the managing partner. When Maggie ran into trouble on the job because it involved a type of research for which she didn't have the background or temperament, she didn't have a relationship with that partner to fall back on when she really needed it.

This time, Maggie came to me for help, and I made her promise to arrange her life so that she would not be in a hurry to decide what was next. Maggie's self-esteem was at an all-time low. But as we reviewed her accomplishments and talents, she began to see that she had a lot to offer the right employer. There was nothing wrong with her skills; they were just different from what had been needed in her last job. Maggie decided to focus on the world of nonprofit organizations. This was where she had been happiest in the past, and now she had both nonprofit and business experience to offer. She worked out a financial plan that would allow her to take her time. It included doing some consulting on a part-time basis.

One of the many people with whom Maggie networked was a former boss who was now working for a nonprofit organization. He remembered her fondly and was happy to hear from her. He invited her in for an interview, and she was offered a job almost immediately. This time, she did not act too quickly. She turned down the job she was offered, which was not the one she wanted. She also told her former boss that she found the work very exciting and was willing to wait until a position came along that she really wanted. A few days later, he asked her to work part-time until they could create a position for her. Maggie agreed but set a time limit of three months. If the position she wanted had not been created by then, she would move on.

Maggie has been working for the organization for several years now. The part-time job turned into the full-time one she wanted. Her colleagues are delighted to have her there, really need her skills, and appreciate her. Because she took the time to figure out what she really wanted and needed to succeed, Maggie was confident about taking this job. It is in a part of the organization that does breakthrough work and attracts people and projects on an international basis, so all of Maggie's interests are met. Her self-esteem has been restored because once again she is succeeding. ●

Taking your time to decide is not the same thing as doing nothing. In fact, you may be very busy, just not rushed to make a decision. Caroline's story offers a good example. Caroline took her time, asked the right questions, and surprised herself with her answers.

Caroline's win

Caroline was let go after twenty years of employment with a major television network. She had grown up at this company, beginning as an administrative assistant and working her way up to assistant producer and, finally, producer.

Of course, Caroline was shocked when she was fired, but she was not really surprised. She had known for some time that things were not going well. As we worked together, she gradually revealed that she thought she really should have left a long time ago.

Caroline took some time off just to rest, visit her family, begin an exercise program, and have some fun. She began some volunteer work that she had wanted to do for a long time. She enjoyed the slower pace and decided never again to allow herself to become consumed by work to the exclusion of other things in her life. In the meantime, she allowed herself to explore both inside and outside the media world. She did a lot of networking and took her time.

A year later, Caroline was still developing the picture of what work she wanted to do in the future, but she was having a lot of success and a great time. Through freelancing, she had produced several commercials, made a videotape for a company, and managed a trade show for the first time. She had enjoyed all three activities. She remarked to me that as a freelancer, she had put herself on the line with these projects as never before, and she had liked it. She had also discovered that she loved variety in her work. As a result, she decided to work for herself instead of looking for a job. She began exploring areas that would use all her production skills, including management of special events.

At our last visit, Caroline said she is convinced that she will never go back to a corporate environment because it is not "her." She is much happier in less formal settings where she is using her strengths and doing the things she is very good at. ●

Caroline is on her way to success and a happier life. She is now grateful for having been let go and is glad she took the time to discover what works best for her.

The path to dreams isn't linear

Once you have clarified what is right for you, it's time to pursue your dreams. Having watched people go through this process thousands of times, I now know that pursuing dreams is indeed a process and not an event. Occasionally things fall into place quickly, but usually they don't. More often, the fulfillment of dreams is preceded by a long period of preparation, a lot of work, and many setbacks.

There seems to be a pattern to this process. If you are like most of my clients, here is what you can expect, more or less. After identifying your dreams (your vision or passions), you will probably come up with several good contacts or possibilities and feel excited about them. You are at the beginning of a process that looks like the bottom of a funnel. It's narrow and small at the beginning, but as you talk to people, more contacts and possibilities open up and your field of potential grows. You are now in the large part of the funnel. If you are in a job search, you will soon have several job offers. Typically, at this point, you may have as many as three offers at the same time.

And then something happens. Every one of the three falls through. I have seen this happen so many times that I now think it is predictable. It usually has nothing to do with you. For example, the first of the three companies reorganizes and eliminates the position. The second company hires someone else (someone who is more experienced, related to the boss, or from inside the company). The third company goes through a major change, the people handling the job applications are transferred out and not immediately replaced, and so on.

This is the most discouraging and dangerous time in the job search process. You are vulnerable not only to your own self-doubts but also to other people's negative comments about the economy and the job market and pressures from your family. You may begin to believe these comments or think you should return to what you were doing before, reduce your dreams and settle for less, or take the first opportunity offered.

This is a time to stick with it; don't quit. It's a time to be expansive; don't contract. The funnel has narrowed again, but all you need to do is open it up. This may feel like starting all over again, but it's not. Even returning to people you talked to earlier is not the same as starting over. You will have come a long way by this time and just need to dig in again. You may think you have exhausted all your leads, but take another look at your lists, open up new avenues for leads, or reframe or redefine what you are pursuing. There are always more people to talk to. If you keep at this process, inevitably the funnel will open up again. The new possibilities that present themselves at this point will probably lead to exactly what you want. I have seen it occur this way often enough that I feel confident in predicting this. It is worth hanging in there and continuing the pursuit for what you really want.

Sometimes, you may have to go through the whole process several times before you land what you want, but usually success comes after the first round of disappointments. Here's what happened to Aaron.

Overcoming panic

When I first met Aaron, he was working as a vice president in his father's real estate development business. He had been doing this work for many years even though it did not excite or interest him much. Leaving a family business is tricky at best. It takes a strong commitment and a willingness to work through all the feelings on everyone's part generated by the decision to leave. Aaron handled all of it admirably, extricated himself, and began a search for work dealing with environmental issues, a subject he had identified as being much closer to his heart.

Aaron's college degree was in chemical engineering, and his work experience with his dad's company had been in marketing. Therefore, he had a great combination of talents to offer the right company. He was also extremely likable, upbeat, and fun to be around.

Aaron was married and the father of a young child. The job search took longer than expected, and he and his wife began to worry. In a state of panic, he grabbed an opportunity with a new company that sounded very risky to me. The company folded within three months, and Aaron was back to his job search again.

The panic resurfaced. Aaron had never formulated a financial backup plan, so he ended up taking a sales job that was underpaid but got him into the environmental industry. He worked hard at the job and was the company's leading salesperson within a year. But because he was underpaid, he had immediately begun looking for another job. When this fact was discovered, Aaron was asked to leave. ●

Aaron's first mistake was panicking when job offers seemed to evaporate. Had he held out longer he might have found his dream job. Sometimes we are shortsighted and think that the most important thing is to get a job, any job, when really the most important thing is to manage our panic. If we can calm ourselves down and remind ourselves that a job search is a process and not an event, we can stay with it long enough to achieve our goals.

A postscript on Aaron

The third time out on the street, Aaron really made use of my support. He talked to me often, and he listened. He knew what he wanted; he just needed to hang in there long enough for it to happen. He came up with a plan for bringing in money to support his family. He began painting houses, which covered the bills and left him time to conduct his job search. On the day I encouraged him to courageously turn down three job offers that were not right for him, his wife talked to me at length and also received my support in remaining calm.

Shortly after that, Aaron got the offer he had really wanted all along. He is now working for an environmental engineering company that is solid and has great growth potential, and he has the salary he wanted. He is working on an M.B.A. degree, having success in his work, and enjoying his job at the company. He reports that it is even better than he had anticipated. His courage and commitment to his dream have paid off. ●

Nine ways to avoid being a victim

Your dreams should be larger than any one job or any particular way you imagine accomplishing them. Jobs can fall through, and there is no one right way to fulfill your dreams. If you pin all your hopes on one job, you are destined to be disappointed. What you love about the job is more important than the job itself. You can always find another job or a different way to do what you love.

Being out of work is unsettling at best. Your self-esteem may plummet and you may feel extremely insecure, regardless of past

---

chart 7
nine ways to avoid being a victim

1. Keep a sense of perspective.
2. Pay attention to your heart.
3. Notice where the ease is and where things flow.
4. Take especially good care of yourself.
5. Take care of your money concerns.
6. Don't spend time with negative people.
7. Give yourself a break.
8. Be flexible.
9. Keep listening and observing.

successes. A period of unemployment is a time to take good care of yourself, to reduce the risk of being vulnerable to bad advice or of making decisions on an emotional basis that you will later regret. If you are unemployed, here are some steps you can take to avoid being a victim and to ensure that you use this time to design a satisfying work situation and a life you will love.

Keep a sense of perspective

Remember that a job interview is not a singles bar experience, a beauty contest, or a courtroom hearing! You are not there to be judged or evaluated. You are there to explore possibilities and *mutually* evaluate with the prospective employer whether the job is a good fit for you. You can and should have the freedom to say "No, thank you" if the vibes are wrong. Trust your intuition.

Pay attention to your heart

Keep noticing what you're drawn to, where your true interests lie, where your energy is. Then feed what interests you, particularly if your interest is sustained for longer than three days. Don't waste your time and energy (or other people's) pursuing leads you have no heart for, just to "keep your options open." Ultimately, these pursuits will drain your energy. Keep focused on what interests you. Then pursue how and where you might do it.

Notice where the ease is and where things flow

Pay attention to where doors open easily, leads are plentiful, lots of ideas are generated, and opportunities keep showing up. Shift your attention and energy away from those areas that seem difficult and immovable. Remember that your major interests can be expressed in different ways.

Take especially good care of yourself

Eat well, exercise regularly, and lay off the alcohol. We all feel full of self-doubt when we're not working. Sometimes in an attempt to handle stress, we eat carelessly, stop exercising, and depend more on alcohol. But far from helping us, all three of these habits contribute to depression and ultimately to even lower self-esteem.

Take care of your money concerns

Generating money is not the same as getting a full-time job. You can generate money in many ways: unemployment insurance, a part-time job, temporary projects, cutting back on expenses, selling things (house, condominium, stocks, bonds, car, furniture, etc.), consulting, part-time sales work, creating your own small business. When you handle the money panic, you create time to truly explore what's next for you.

Don't spend time with negative people

Avoid all those friends and relatives who have nothing good to say about the economy or the industry you worked in or who are grim about the future. You will probably be finding it hard enough to manage your own thoughts; you don't need this negative input. Instead, spend time with optimistic people who are busy making things happen, not moaning about what isn't happening.

Give yourself a break

Use this time to think about where you want to put your life energy. Maybe this is the time to return to school, to start that business you've been dreaming about for years, to move, to get into another field, or to turn a hobby into a living. Keep remembering that there is plenty of work out there that needs doing. There are many opportunities to create new jobs and careers.

Be flexible

A job can be very limiting and constraining. Maybe you should think of yourself as someone who finds or generates interesting projects rather than someone who is job hunting. Trading the security of a regular paycheck for the excitement of work you love (and perhaps even more money than the regular paycheck) may be well worth it.

Keep listening and observing

Ask yourself: What's wanted, needed, and missing that I can match with my talent, energy, and enthusiasm? This is a better way to approach a job search than through the newspaper. Reading the want ads to find a job that fits you often leads to despair. Don't rely on the ads to define the direction of your job search. Instead, be proactive. Ask yourself: What are the gaps that I can fill? That way you will be in charge and will have a focus for your search. Then, get appointments with people in hiring positions and open up conversations for possibility. One result could be a job created just for you.

As you can see, being unemployed doesn't automatically mean being a victim. If you use these nine suggested ways to handle yourself, you will be empowered through this temporary stage in your working life. Remember that even when you are unemployed, regardless of how it appears, you are in charge of your life.

key 1   Reveal what's true for you
key 2   Reclaim your personal power
key 3   Express your commitment
key 4   Surround yourself with support

Questions to ask yourself

• What's the "blessing in disguise" in my current situation?

• How can I best use this time away from my regular work routine?

• Is this the right time to "go for" my dream?

Action steps to take

• Form a support group, even if it's with only one other unemployed person. Just make sure that you focus on producing results and not on complaining. Set daily and weekly targets and goals. Help each other keep promises. Communicate with group members regularly and often.

• Find at least one person who went through an extended period of unemployment and is now happy in his or her new work. Find out what helped this person hold out for the right job.

• Get a part-time job in order to have somewhere to go, something to do, people to be with, and some money coming in.

I'm in heaven. I'm making more money, working half the time, and I'm free to develop work that really interests me.

—a newly self-employed client

chapter 11
great mondays may mean self-employment

When you have clarified what you want to do with your work and life, you may find that the answer is to have a business of your own. You may decide to work by yourself, work with a partner, or build a business that employs others. During my seventeen years of self-employment, I have done all three—and I have made just about every mistake possible. I am, after all, the person who, after two years of being in business, called her accountant and asked, "Allan, what's profit?" To his everlasting credit, he didn't laugh. If I could be that naive about business and still succeed, so can you.

People decide to be self-employed for a number of different reasons. Do any of these apply to you?

- You've decided that self-employment is the only way you can fulfill your passion.

- You want to carry out an idea and have decided you can't do it in your current work situation.

- You're someone no one else can manage.

- You like the idea of unlimited earnings, dependent solely on what you produce.

- You value independence and freedom over security.

- You want to be in charge.

- You believe you have little choice in the matter because you are too old and too experienced to find another challenging position within a company.

- You resent the lack of appreciation and opportunity at your company.

- You're being laid off, don't know what to do next, and need to earn some money right away.

- It's in your blood.

Sometimes people fall into self-employment without planning it but discover that it fits well, as Martin did.

The computer expert

Martin is a software developer who was let go from his company during a downsizing. He didn't consider self-employment and planned to look for another full-time job. In the meantime, in order to keep money flowing, he began to do freelance work as a consultant. When he attended my career workshop, Martin identified two career goals: to be known as a software expert and to be a writer-commentator. He did not specify whether either of these involved being employed by someone else.

As time went on, Martin's reputation spread and his workload increased. He joined my entrepreneurs' support group to stay on track. He also met a number of computer specialists who were in the same situation, and together they decided to start a computer users' support group. The response was very good. Then Martin started a newsletter. His humor, wisdom, and writing skills made it an immediate success, and his goal of becoming a writer and commentator was realized.

Next, Martin began teaching computer skills. After two years of steady work and with assignments lined up for the third year, Martin acknowledged that he was successfully self-employed and really happy. He had found several venues in which to be a commentator, was considered an expert, and loved the variety in his work as well as the independence it afforded him. He decided to stick with his new business venture and forget about looking for a job. ●

Where are you on the passion scale?

The number one requirement for succeeding at your own business is to do something you are passionate about. You can count on having difficulties; they are just part of the game. You had better care about what you are doing; otherwise, it's too easy to give up.

It usually takes many work hours to get a business off the ground. There are people, such as the client quoted at the beginning of this chapter, who work less and earn more when they start a business, but they're the exception, not the rule, especially at first. Don't start a business with the idea that you will be able to play golf whenever you want. It's true that when you work for yourself you can often design a flexible lifestyle that allows for spending time with children, playing golf, or getting your hair cut in the middle of the week, but these are by-products of a healthy business, not the central focus. It takes concentration and energy to establish a new business. However, if you're excited about doing so, there's nothing better. Therefore, in addition to being passionate about having a business of your own, it's best to choose a product or service you are passionate about.

On a scale of 1 to 10, with 1 being "It's boring" and 10 being "I'm crazy about it," how do you feel about the product or service you plan to offer?

0	5	10
It's boring	It's okay	I'm crazy about it

If your score is 5 or below, keep looking until you find something you can honestly be excited about. If it's 7 to 9, ask yourself this: What's missing? What would make it a 10?

Charles is someone who built his business around a passion that he almost didn't recognize because it was such a natural part of his life.

"Stuff" becomes a business

Charles has always loved "stuff"—jewelry, antiques, furniture, artwork, clothes. The passion for collecting is in his blood. From early childhood, he has loved looking at, learning about, and collecting objects. He also loves to sell things and make deals. His father collected antiques and wrote books about them. The love of "things" was all around Charles.

I met Charles when he was twenty-three years old, after he had had several unsuccessful job experiences. Here was a guy who was having a hard time finding a place to get started in his working life. Charles kept trying to find a fit in a job working for other people. Whether he was selling hot dogs, working in a cigar store, or selling jewelry, he inevitably ended up bored and restless and quit after a short time. Finally, he gave up searching for a job and started his own business.

He began by helping people clean out their basements. Charles worked with great integrity, leaving the basements "broom clean." He took pride in his work, but he especially loved the "treasures" he often found, which he later sold for his clients. This work evolved into the business he has today, buying and selling people's estates. It's a natural fit for him. He is not bored. He loves being his own boss. He takes great care of his customers and gets to make use of his talent for finding treasures as well as his love of "wheeling and dealing." He uses talents and interests so natural to him that he almost overlooked them. ●

Just as important as choosing a business you are passionate about is making sure your business addresses an unmet need or fills a gap. Remember those questions to ask yourself: What's wanted and needed? What's missing? Also ask yourself what it is that you know best or do better than anyone else. What do you care more strongly about than most people do? When you have found your answer, turn it into a business, as Judy did.

Ahead of her time

Judy had cooked vegetarian food for several years for a religious community. When she left the community, she was at a loss for a way to support herself and began working as a waitress. Food was what she knew best, and Judy was passionate about making healthy eating choices. Even though there were not very many people interested in vegetarian choices when I first met Judy, she decided to turn this into her work.

She began by cooking for people and counseling them on selecting health-supporting foods. She went to people's homes and taught them how to read labels and identify unwholesome ingredients. She took people shopping and introduced them to health food stores they had never visited before. Gradually, she stopped cooking and began teaching cooking classes, focusing on easy-to-prepare recipes. She designed a course to help people get unhooked from diets and still manage their weight. She wrote articles and columns. She hooked up with several chiropractors to advise their patients and gave talks to organizations and on radio and television.

It was hard at first because Judy was way ahead of the times. Even so, right from the beginning, she was able to support herself. She created a small industry out of her passion, her abilities, and what she saw that people needed. Today, her work is almost mainstream. ●

Judy's business proves that it's possible to support yourself by providing unusual services. Nan's successful business is another example. After spending twenty years in the corporate communications department of an international company, Nan left to start a temporary placement business supplying companies with graphic designers and writers instead of secretaries. She began in the mid-1980s and met an unfilled need at a time when the outsourcing of many services was just beginning to be common. Because of this growing trend, it is easier to be self-employed now than it has been at any other time I can remember. Chart 8 presents some strategies if you choose to be self-employed.

Fifteen ways to avoid the common pitfalls of self-employment

I have been leading a monthly support group for entrepreneurs for more than fifteen years. The success rate for members of the group has been the opposite of that for most business owners—90 to 95 percent of my clients have been successful. It is no accident. They manage to avoid the common pitfall of being isolated, instead surrounding themselves with support. What are other pitfalls to avoid? The following pages describe fifteen of them and suggest ways to avoid them. They fall into three categories: managing money; running the business; and managing yourself. You will recognize the four keys to finding fulfillment at work in many of them. The first four suggestions have to do with managing money.

Learn to cope with cash flow problems

It's important for any business owner to learn to view the ups and downs of money as cash flow problems, not personal failings. This took me a long time to do. Most of us are used to regular paychecks, and not having them can be unnerving and disheartening. It can

chart 8
fifteen ways to avoid the common pitfalls of self-employment

Managing Money
1. Learn to cope with cash flow problems.
2. Keep up with your billing.
3. Create a "cash cow."
4. Take care of your taxes.

Running the Business
5. Face up to difficult business issues.
6. Market, market, market, and sell, sell, sell.
7. Build a strong core business.
8. Start small.
9. Put structure into your business.
10. Get started.

Managing Yourself
11. Take vacations.
12. When you get scared, get into action.
13. Avoid distractions and take yourself seriously.
14. Set up a support system.
15. Stick with it.

feel as if we are failing when there is little or no money coming in, when in fact we might only be in the "desert" phase of a "desert and rain forest" cycle. It can really help to put one month's lack of money into the context of a cash flow problem. Then, the important thing to do is to keep going. Sow seeds for the future. It is also important not to confuse a cash flow problem with the problem of not generating enough income to pay the bills. That's a different issue. If you are not earning enough money, you will need to take other steps, such as reducing expenses or creating a "cash cow."

Keep up with your billing

Bill for your services right away and collect as soon as possible. Regular billing and regular collecting will keep your cash flow as even as possible and will reduce the risk of defaults in payment. Sadly, history shows that if you are not paid within two months of billing, your chances of collecting grow dimmer every day, no matter how well you did the job. This is something to stay on top of. In addition, whenever possible, get a deposit on your work. Again, this will help with the cash flow.

Create a "cash cow"

A "cash cow" is some service or product that you can sell easily and regularly, in contrast with those services or products that take a long time to come to fruition. It pays the rent. It allows you to sleep at night.

If you are doing business with corporations, you will discover that it often takes many months to land a contract. You may also be surprised to find that people who are salaried generally do not think of their time as money. As a business owner, you will. Another good reason for having a "cash cow" is that it will allow you to see progress and be rewarded for your efforts as you go along. Most of us don't do well with delayed gratification, especially if it's delayed a long time.

Take care of your taxes

Be honest and pay on time, end of story. Do *not* fool with the Internal Revenue Service. The IRS can be relentless in getting its money, including interest and penalties. With interest and penalties added on to what you originally owe, you can end up paying almost twice the original amount. Just bite the bullet and pay your taxes religiously. It's worth it. You'll have peace of mind and keep your business safe.

If for some reason you can't pay your taxes, communicate with the Internal Revenue Service right away. Do *not* ignore the IRS; it will not ignore you, I promise. This is a serious issue and can set you back for years if you don't deal with it properly. Early in the life of my business an accountant friend gave me bad advice on my taxes and I ended up owing money. I didn't have the money at the time, and it took me several years to catch up. I also had two clients who almost lost their businesses because they didn't pay their taxes on time. It's draining to pay for back debts, so the best thing to do is handle your taxes right away. Hire a competent and honest accountant to help you stay on track.

The following six suggestions will help you avoid pitfalls in running the business.

Face up to difficult business issues

Don't ignore other thorny issues such as leases, legal questions, bookkeeping, payroll, and insurance or dump them on other people, especially in the beginning. You will need to hire professionals to help you with some of these things, but doing so does not let you off the hook. Ultimately, you are still the one who is responsible, so it is not wise to put your head in the sand. It is best to know something about each of these areas. I remember walking into a lawyer's office and dumping my twenty-seven-page office lease on his desk. I told him I couldn't possibly understand it and I wanted him to handle it. He said that no matter what he did, I should read the entire document myself so I would know what was in it. It was great advice. I did read the lease carefully, and it gave me a better sense of security whenever I talked to the landlord or had to negotiate with him. Read your leases, agreements, and insurance papers.

Market, market, market, and sell, sell, sell

Often, new business owners are shocked to discover how much time and energy is required to generate work and keep it flowing. In the beginning, it can take as much as 80 percent of your time. This can be a hard lesson to learn, especially for those who find marketing distasteful or unfamiliar. For every small business owner, it's a tough balancing act to market the business while also providing the service. Small businesses undergo "desert and rain forest" cycles as a result. It's "Oh, no—no business!" Market, market, market. "Oh no—too much business!" No marketing. "Oh, no—no business!" And so on. The trick is to plan a way to continue marketing your business even when you are busy or learn to enjoy the down times, using them to rest and be creative, and then market again. As a business owner, you also need to learn how to sell your particular product or service. Hard as it may be to believe, no one else will care as much about it as you do. It is worthwhile to take a course in selling if you have never sold before. One unsuccessful business owner with whom I worked ignored my advice to learn how to sell directly to customers and decided to use only mailings. His business failed because he could not afford direct mail marketing and because he missed out on the valuable feedback he would have gained during conversations with potential and established customers.

Build a strong core business

Don't go in too many directions at once, especially in the beginning. It is good to create several products or related services; however, you don't want to begin three different businesses at the same time. I know there are successful people who own many businesses, but I'll bet if you examined their histories you would discover that they got one of the businesses running smoothly before they tackled another one. Grow your business like you would a tree: with strong roots in the ground first and a firm trunk before you add branches.

Start small

Many entrepreneurs think they need to have what they just left behind: a plush office, secretarial support, beautiful marketing materials, and fancy equipment. This is a mistake. These are all ego needs, not business needs. You don't need to spend a lot of money to get started; you just need to provide a good product or service. Begin in your home if at all possible. Don't take on the added expense of supporting an office unless you really have to. And don't put anyone on the payroll until you are sure you really want to and can handle it financially. It's a big responsibility to have someone else depending on you for income. Hire people as subcontractors or temporary workers until you are sure that having employees is the right next step.

Don't spend money on flashy marketing materials until you really know what your business is (and maybe not even then). You'll need to line up customers and get to work in order to figure out what your business is really all about. Don't even hire support help in the beginning unless you have to. Doing everything yourself at this stage allows you to design the business the way you want it to be. Morever, it's fun, gives you an education that will serve you well later, and saves you money.

Put structure into your business

You may be someone who prefers to work from noon to eight o'clock in the evening instead of from nine to five. That's fine; just structure your time so you really work during those hours. This is all part of taking yourself seriously as a business owner and learning to be productive on your own. Set daily targets and monthly and yearly goals. Make it a game. Plan rewards you will give yourself when you achieve your targets and goals.

Get started

Don't worry about writing a business plan unless you need to borrow money to get started. Many people allow themselves to become overwhelmed by this task and never get off the ground. The most important thing is to get customers so you can begin to figure out what this business is that you're creating. You will learn a lot along the way, and each discovery will change the shape of your business. A year later, it may not look anything like your first concept of it. Of course, you should do your homework, but don't put off starting because you don't have a business plan. Just go get clients.

The remaining five suggestions will help you avoid common pitfalls in managing yourself.

Take vacations

In the beginning stages of your business, you'll need to do everything yourself and probably will not mind doing it. After all, you love what you're doing, and the business is your own. You are designing and building it the way you have always wanted it to be. Add to this some fear about stopping and you may end up letting too much time go by without taking a vacation or break. What I and my clients have discovered over the years is that taking a break from the business always helps, despite any disruption that might result. The disruption is never as bad as we think it will be, and any drop in income is usually made up quickly.

When you get scared, get into action

Looking at a blank calendar or a growing pile of debts is not just scary—it's terrifying. This is the time to pick up the telephone and get into action. Almost anything you do will help. The only thing that won't help is inaction; that will only dig a deeper hole. Energy out brings energy in. Do what you know to do: send out fliers or letters, give talks, call former clients, attend meetings and conferences, write articles, make cold calls. Almost any activity will help, but talking to people is usually the least expensive and best approach.

Avoid distractions and take yourself seriously

Some people are easily distracted by television, the chance to sleep late, friends who are not working, and family members (especially children). It's hard to say no and discipline yourself. If, in addition, you have a partner or spouse who refers to your work as your "cute little business," you need to find ways to take the business more seriously yourself and make sure everyone around you does too. For example, get up in the morning and get dressed; don't work in your pajamas. Have a separate telephone line for the business. When you record a greeting on the answering machine, don't have music or crying babies in the background. Don't answer the business line after working hours. Create your own work space, and don't allow other family members to use it. All these things signal your serious intentions.

Set up a support system

It's important to enlist lots of support to help you celebrate your successes and handle the down times, especially if you work alone and/or from home. I started a support group for entrepreneurs that has met once a month since the mid-1980s. It is unlike the usual business groups in that it is small, no one is in competition with anyone else, and discussion of personal topics is encouraged. Anything is fair game—family problems, marketing, employee issues, money fears, triumphs. Everyone looks forward to the meetings. There are many different groups out there to join; some offer technical information about running a business, and others focus on generating leads. Whether they are formal or informal, large or small, such groups are a good form of support. The important thing is to get out of your house or office (and your mind) and enter into conversation with other people. Otherwise, it can be lonely and you can get stuck in your own thinking.

Stick with it

Make a commitment to being on your own. Don't brush up your résumé and periodically run off for job interviews or tell people you are working for yourself "unless something better comes along." This diffuses your energy and confuses people. Make a commitment. You can set a date to reevaluate your decision—for instance, in one year. Until then, focus only on making the business work. It's okay to quit later if it's not the right thing for you. Amber is someone who did both of these things in the right way.

Self-employment leads to a job

Amber lost her job as a buyer for a major retail chain when the company reorganized and downsized. She had grown up in the company and was shocked to be out on the street after fifteen years of dedicated service.

Because she was in no hurry to work for another company right away and had often thought about having a business of her own, Amber decided to work as an independent consultant to retail stores. To get started, she connected with the vast network she had established in her job and let everyone know she was available.

She made a commitment to being self-employed, and business started pouring in. Over the next three years, Amber spent eight months in France consulting for a store, helped an artist in China bring several products to market, served as an account manager for one company, helped a client design and open a showroom, and accompanied clients on buying trips. All these assignments were interesting and lucrative, but Amber was not sure whether she wanted to continue on her own. Something was missing. Then, out of the blue, she was offered a job running a catalog division for a small retail company. She called to tell me she had decided to take the job because it was exciting; it was based in New York, where she wanted to be; and she would be working with a team of people she really liked. In her eyes, the job represented one of the last great retail opportunities. She believed she would be happier working for a company than working on her own.

Amber gave it her best when she was independent and did not diffuse her energy or dilute her effectiveness by job hunt-

ing at the same time. The job offer she received was sponta-
neous and resulted from her good work. Even though Amber
now believes she is better suited to working for a company, she
values every minute of the time she spent self-employed:
"It was humbling, and I learned so much, mostly about
myself." ●

It's okay to decide not to build a big business. Although we are
barraged with the message that bigger is better, that is not true for
everyone. Owning or working for a big company sometimes dis-
tances people from the heart or center of their work. There are
other ways to grow, such as increasing the depth, quality, or scope
of your work. You can decide to focus on those instead.

Working on your own is not easy, but all work has its challenges. No work is free from stress. Whether you work for yourself
or for someone else, you have to decide what you are willing to put
up with. Despite all the times I have worried about income, I have
always been more willing to put up with financial uncertainty than
to relinquish the freedom to make my own choices and design my
own work. You need to know what's most important to you.

If you decide that self-employment is for you, you will find that
being on your own is full of challenges but is also enormously
rewarding. It is great to call the shots. Once you have become successful at it, you may never consider working for anyone else again.

At this point in the book, I hope you are actively using the four
keys to improve your current work situation, move to an exciting
new work environment, or become happily self-employed. But what
if this is not true for you and instead you're still floundering or
stalled? Read on to discover what to do if nothing is working right.

key 1   Reveal what's true for you
key 2   Reclaim your personal power
key 3   Express your commitment
key 4   Surround yourself with support

Questions to ask yourself

- If I have been thinking about starting a business of my own, what am I waiting for?

- How could I get my first client or customer? Who would it be?

- Where in my home could I set up my work space?

Action steps to take

- Figure out what you would need to get started in business: telephone (with answering machine or voice mail), computer, printer, modem, fax machine, business cards, and stationery. That's probably it, unless you are selling products. How much would this cost you? Break the total down into monthly amounts. Don't forget to consider the possibility of leasing or renting equipment.

- Figure out how much money you need to make each year. Start with the necessities, and then add a few extras. Include taxes and health insurance costs, and be sure to allow for some vacation or sick time. Finally, add the cost of running your business, including a profit. Now divide this total by twelve to see how much you need to bring in each month. Break it down by days and hours, too.

- Interview two or three business owners who love being self-employed and consider themselves successful. (Make sure these are people you will not be in competition with.) Ask them how they got started, what they like and dislike about self-employment, what mistakes they have made, and what obstacles they have met and how they have overcome them.

part four
staying on course

Life is a lot better on the other side of addiction.

—everyone who has overcome an addiction

chapter 12

when nothing works

Do any of the following descriptions fit you?

- You're always being told you have great potential but you never live up to it.

- You know what to do but just can't seem to get started.

- You can't seem to complete any career-related assignments.

- You take one step forward in your work and then fall back two.

- You're too tired to do much of anything except make it through the day.

- You end up being fired from most jobs or consistently have problems with bosses or co-workers.

Six personal problems that can hold people back

If any of the preceding statements sounds familiar, maybe it's time to stop focusing on work and begin to examine the rest of your life to see what's preventing you from achieving your dreams. Maybe it's not a career problem. Maybe it's a personal problem. Often the real problem is not what it first appears to be. Whenever I work with a client who can't follow through on action steps we have both agreed on, I suspect that he or she is struggling with a personal problem that hasn't been revealed yet.

In my experience, six personal problems have the potential to deter people from fulfilling their dreams for their work and life (see Chart 9 below). Managing a demanding job, taking care of a home and relationships, finding time for recreation, and, on top of it all, pursuing dreams for the future take enormous energy, both physical and psychological. If you also have personal problems that are distracting or fatiguing, it is difficult, at best, to make progress. It may even be impossible unless you take care of the problems first. Otherwise, it's like driving a car with one foot on the gas pedal and one foot on the brake.

chart 9
six personal problems that can hold people back

1. Illness
2. Low self-esteem
3. Depression
4. Addiction
5. Unhappy or abusive relationships
6. Unresolved trauma

If you are experiencing any of these problems, don't give up on your dreams. You can still accomplish them, but you will have to make resolving the problems your first priority.

Illness

If you have exciting goals but are so fatigued that you can't ever seem to get going, you may be wondering, "What's wrong with me?" Not every block to success is psychological. Maybe you have a physical problem and need to be kinder to yourself and demand less. A debilitating illness, such as infection with the Epstein-Barr virus, can sap your energy. It's important to make sure that you're healthy. When you're sick, it's unwise to start something new or make a major decision. Your only task at such a time is to take care of yourself and get well. When your energy and health return, you can get going again.

Some health issues are acute but transitory: once you are diagnosed and treated, you are on the road to recovery and can get right back on track with your goals. But chronic health problems—those that are persistent or recurrent over a long period—can have such a profound effect that you have to redesign your life around them. My clients have confronted a variety of chronic illnesses—diabetes, AIDS, Crohn's disease, cancer, environmental illness—that demanded a lot of attention from them and influenced their work and life decisions for the future.

On the basis of what my clients have shown me, I can assure you that even though a chronic illness can keep you from carrying out some of your plans, you can design your work and life to still include exciting opportunities. Patty's experience with environmental illness is an example.

A new life

Patty was a successful vice president of sales and in her mid-thirties when I met her. During a career workshop, she tearfully revealed that she had been diagnosed with environmental illness, a condition thought to be caused by extreme sensitivity to allergens and characterized by chronic exhaustion and weakness. Like many illnesses, it is exacerbated by stress. Patty loved her job even though it was demanding and placed her under a great deal of pressure. She commonly worked sixty-hour weeks and was in and out of airplanes and hotel rooms filled with allergens. Patty finally admitted that she usually ended up sleeping all weekend to recover from a week of work and that it was too much for her to handle.

Everyone in the workshop encouraged Patty to leave her job, but she had a hard time letting go. Moreover, her boss valued her so highly that he was willing to do almost anything to keep her. So after the workshop, Patty first tried reducing her travel schedule and working from home several days a week. That helped, but it wasn't enough. After several months, she finally admitted that she needed a complete break from the stress and a long period of rest. She left her job and gave herself six months to rest and decide what to do next.

Two months later, feeling much better, Patty took a long trip to Europe, with no negative consequences. When she returned, she focused on taking good care of herself through nutrition and exercise. She began feeling better and better. Gradually, she gathered the energy to explore different careers.

Her new direction fell into place over a period of many months. Patty started a business working from home as a wellness coach, helping people take good care of themselves. This role builds on her personal experience and the research and study she has done on wellness, and it makes use of her expertise in sales as well. It is a good fit, and she is excited. Most important, Patty's new business allows her to work in a less stressful environment, both physically and psychologically, and she is much healthier. ●

If you are tired all the time, have flare-ups of a chronic disease, are recovering from surgery, or are undergoing radiation treatments or chemotherapy, give yourself a break. Don't expect to take on major life changes until you feel better. And if you don't know what's wrong with you but suspect something physical, go to a doctor before you decide it's just psychological.

Low self-esteem

If you have problems with low self-esteem, it may be hard for you to get excited about any future possibilities because your inner voices are screaming:

"I can't do it."

"Nothing I've done has ever worked out right."

"I never get what I want anyway."

"I don't deserve it."

"I'm not good enough."

"If they only really knew . . . ."

"I don't know how to do it, and I'll never figure it out."

Even if you quiet the voices long enough to feel your excitement, you may find yourself paralyzed and unable to take action. If that's the case, you need to work on shoring up your self-esteem before concentrating on accomplishing your goals.

If you have low self-esteem, your internal scales are already tipped by self-criticism. You find yourself unable to handle any negative feedback, no matter how minor, even though intellectually you know that everyone needs criticism to grow. It's even likely that you hear praise with a high degree of skepticism and find yourself unable to accept it.

If you suffer from low self-esteem, don't despair. It's not a permanent condition; you can do something about it. Take on increasing your self-esteem as a goal. For instance, work with a psychotherapist to get to the root causes, attend self-esteem workshops and seminars, or read books and listen to tapes. Sometimes low self-esteem results from gaps in knowledge or experience. If this is the case, *do* something about it. Find a mentor, classes, or the experience you need to fill the gap. Here's what Mark did.

Mark leaves home

Mark was in his mid-thirties and had worked from his home as a freelance journalist for many years when he married. Although he had been successful enough to have many articles published, Mark had never earned a great deal of money. Mark's wife, Carol, had an exceptionally high income as a television and movie producer, so the two of them agreed that Mark would continue to work at home. Whenever Carol was working on a project, Mark would take over the household chores.

But then a baby came, and Mark had three jobs: the house-work, his writing, and childcare. In addition, he and Carol were yearning to fulfill a long-held dream of writing and producing movies together. To move them closer to their goal, Mark changed his focus from journalism to screenplay writing. They knew it might take a long time to break into Hollywood, but they were willing to wait. In the meantime, because of the demands involved in caring for the baby, Mark was suffering from not having enough consistent time for writing. He was also dealing with the harsh reality of receiving many rejections for his screenplays. Mark's self-esteem was at a new low.

Then an opportunity fell into Mark's lap to work at an advertising agency for a short time writing commercials. The writing came easily to him. He had a great sense of humor and had already learned how to write scenes. Mark was instrumental in helping the advertising agency land a big contract.

Because they wanted to keep alive their dream of making movies together, Mark and Carol came to work with me to plan their future. I was amazed. I had known Mark for many years, and now he was like a new person. He was filled with enthusiasm and confidence. Having success as an employee, being well paid, and feeling valuable to a team had made all the difference. Mark summarized it when he said, "I worked alone in my home for too long." It had been a great experience for him to go to an office each day and earn a good paycheck for his efforts.

Mark is now more committed than ever to becoming a successful screenwriter. He is developing several projects and has a Hollywood agent. And he is confident that he will be able to sell himself when he and Carol make their planned move to Los Angeles to further their work and life goals. ●

Mark filled in the gaps in his experience and gained a huge increase in self-esteem. If you have gaps in experience or education, stop moaning about them. Take steps to fill them—go to school, hire a consultant or tutor, get the right job. You are not condemned to feeling inadequate for the rest of your life.

Depression

When I work with people who are never enthusiastic about future possibilities and are unable to follow through on assignments, I ask them whether they're ever excited about anything. If the answer is no, there may be a problem with depression.

There are two common forms of depression, chronic and situational. If you are suffering from chronic depression, you have felt this way for a long time, perhaps most of your life. If you are experiencing situational depression, you will be able to date its beginning to a specific and perhaps recent incident, such as the death of a parent or the breakup of a relationship. Today, lots of help is available for both kinds of depression, and there is plenty of hope for recovery. Therapy, perhaps combined with some medication, can make all the difference. I have many clients who have been able to get on with their lives after getting such help. If you handle the depression, your enthusiasm will surface again, and you will have the energy needed for growth and change.

First things first

Brad, a man in his early forties, came to see me shortly after leaving his corporate job. He filled me in on his past work history as a successful, well-paid vice president of sales. After fifteen years with the same company, he was frustrated by a lack of direction and decided he wanted to be on his own. He and his boss agreed to disagree, and Brad left at the end of the year with no plan in place.

When he came to see me, shortly after leaving, he was optimistic and excited. He loved his newfound freedom and was exploring many opportunities for a business of his own. Finally, he chose a business he was enthusiastic about, but he couldn't seem to get it off the ground. He kept finding reasons not to start and began to question whether he had made the right choice.

No suggestions, advice, or encouragement from me seemed to make a difference, and Brad withdrew more and more as time went on. He became increasingly unwilling to take risks, and his attitude became more negative and pessimistic. Finally, he began talking about his unhappy childhood, his past divorce, the recent death of a close friend, and bouts of low self-esteem he had been experiencing for years despite his successes.

Brad finally decided that the decision to leave his job had been a good one but the change had brought old problems to the surface, and the best thing he could do right now was get into therapy. I agreed. We both knew he needed to fill up inside before he would have the energy required to build a business. We decided to meet again after he had completed some work with the therapist. ●

Brad's emotional life was in need of attention. Personal work needed to come before career work.

Addiction

Any addiction (to drugs, alcohol, food, cigarettes, gambling, and so on) depletes your energy and undermines your goals. What are the clues that you have an addiction? There are the hangovers, especially on Monday mornings; restlessness until the next "hit"; planning your life around the addiction; edginess, paranoia, or violent outbursts; mental preoccupation; denial; poor judgment; mediocre performance reviews; possibly blackouts; and endless promises to yourself that you'll quit or cut down tomorrow. It's exhausting. I know from personal experience. My addiction was alcohol. It took me a long time to recognize and admit that I had a serious problem.

You know you are in the throes of a full-blown addiction when stopping looks as if it would be a disaster. People who are not addicted can easily stop forever and not just for limited periods of time. Before I quit, I believed that alcohol was the source of my good ideas and the only way I could relax, get a good night's sleep, or be rewarded for all my hard work. Quitting seemed ridiculous and impossible.

When you are addicted, you can't imagine life being better without the drug, only worse. The full price you have been paying for your addiction becomes apparent only after you've stopped. Admitting the addiction is the hardest part. Usually, people around you, including employees and co-workers, are fooled or cover up for you. They are doing you no favor. Maybe you'll have to hit bottom before you change. I hope not. I hope that your wish not to harm your family, friends, and work is enough to move you to find help, or that your problems with self-esteem will propel you into action. We all have an internal voice that tells us when something is terribly wrong, warning us when there's a breach of integrity with our bodies. That warning voice, no matter how small, is your opportunity for change. Trust that inner voice; put it on loud-speaker. Here's how Bonnie did it.

Bonnie's victory

Bonnie and I met for the first time in the fall. She was a beautiful woman in her early thirties, full of pep and enthusiasm but difficult to be with. Her energy had a nervous quality to it. She seemed "wired."

Bonnie talked rapidly and nonstop about her life and what she wanted for herself. She was happily married to a successful and prominent man. She was the mother of three children; she had many friends, a full social life, a beautiful home, and more than enough money; and she was active in volunteer work. It appeared that she had everything anyone could want, but she said she felt as if something were missing, "something of my own." We set a date to start working together, and as we said good-bye, Bonnie hinted at past addictions and destructive patterns of behavior and her fear that they were reappearing.

A few days before her next appointment, Bonnie called to say she was not yet ready to begin. She was entering an addiction recovery program full-time and would not be able to focus on work for a while. She said she would call me when she had her feet on the ground. True to her word, she called nine months later.

When I met with Bonnie again, she revealed that she was now totally "clean" for the first time in fifteen years. She looked wonderful. She was now clear about the role addiction had played in her life and the way it had negatively affected all her relationships. What emerged as she talked was a peaceful woman with abundant energy and a great love for life. She was easy to be with. The work she had done to foster her own personal growth had spilled over into her family, and everyone had benefited. As a result, Bonnie's self-esteem had gone up by about a thousand percent since the last time I saw her. She had completed the homework assigned to her and had several great ideas about work she wanted to pursue. We had a good session, one that would not have been possible had she not first taken care of the addiction. It would always have held her back. •

Today, when someone has great potential but just can't seem to get it together, I often suspect a hidden addiction. If you have the tiniest suspicion that you have an addiction, at least get an evaluation. You're lucky to be alive at a time when there is increased awareness of addiction as a disease and so many forms of help are available, including books and tapes; one-on-one or group counseling; self-help groups such as Alcoholics Anonymous, Overeaters Anonymous, and Debtors Anonymous; programs at hospitals and private institutions; and medical approaches.

If you find yourself in a rage at the thought of giving up alcohol or any other addiction, rationalizing why it isn't necessary to quit, or telling yourself you can cut down anytime you want to, find someone to talk to who knows about addiction. Cutting down is rarely an option; quitting is the only answer. Call for information or visit a meeting or institution before deciding what's best for you. If you don't like the first meeting or place you visit, try another one. They can be very different even while being committed to the same goals. The initial visit is usually hard to make alone, so you might want to ask a friend or family member to go with you, or someone you know who has struggled with an addiction and successfully overcome it. If you have tried and failed before, don't give up; try again. I, for one, can tell you that the world is a much better place on the other side of addiction.

Unhappy or abusive relationships

It is debilitating and emotionally consuming to be in an unhappy relationship, especially an abusive one. At best, it is difficult to concentrate. Your energy is drained, and your self-esteem is ultimately destroyed. People who abuse others, whether emotionally or physically, are driven in part by insecurity, regardless of how self-assured they may appear. They perceive another's success as a threat to them and fear they will lose control of the other person. An abusive partner will deliberately and repeatedly sabotage your efforts, so your progress ends up being one step forward and two back. Nothing will help except getting out of the relationship or altering it so there is no more abuse, period. If you are in this situation, that's the work you need to do first, before taking on new work or life goals. In fact, it should be your primary goal.

One reward of getting out of a destructive relationship is that you can no longer blame that person for all your failures. You may be surprised to discover the ways *you* stop yourself, but now you will have the opportunity to confront your personal demons and handle them.

Some people can extricate themselves from bad relationships with the help of family and friends, but often additional support from professionals, such as psychotherapists, counselors, and lawyers, is needed. Don't be stubborn about trying to do it alone. It could be dangerous for you, and at a time like this, you need support. Remember, too, just as with addictions, the situation today is more hopeful than ever before. Abuse is now openly talked about, help is available, and seeking help in such a situation is considered a sign of strength.

Unresolved trauma

Some people experience terrible traumatic events that end up dominating their lives. When that happens, they have *become* their trauma. You can see it in their bodies. They look grief stricken, or they act and dress as they did twenty years before, as if their lives were frozen at some point in time. Something from the past has not been healed.

At some point, we all need to put the past in the past, look forward, and get on with our lives, whether it's to dedicate our lives as a memorial to the people we lost or to invent a new life for ourselves. The best way to do this is to get some help from a qualified professional, perhaps a psychotherapist or a spiritual advisor, because forgiveness is one of the major tools of healing. There is also a growing library of books that address these topics, as well as workshops and seminars.

I will never forget one person I met who within the first few minutes of meeting began talking about the death of one of her children. It had been a terrible tragedy. As she continued, it became clear that she and her husband had been unable to put their lives back together after this event, which had occurred more than twenty years earlier. Every year or so, they had moved to a new location or a new job in an effort to find "something." She was unable to find any peace. She had not found a new purpose for her life or a way to channel her grief or heal her heart.

I have noticed that people who experienced the trauma of abuse in their childhood and have not resolved it in some way have a tendency to be very defensive. Direct communications and criti-

cism of any kind are heard as abusive attacks, and they immediately distance themselves. It is almost impossible to communicate
with them at these times. With some people who have experienced
abuse, communication is difficult almost all the time. These behaviors need to be addressed before any measurable progress can be
made toward meeting goals.

If you have any of the personal problems described here, you
can still experience success. We all know people who have overcome tremendous obstacles. But if you do not take care of the
problem, at some point it *will* catch up with you, sabotaging your
success and undermining your satisfaction and fulfillment. Sometimes people can work on these problems at the same time they
pursue their dreams, but this is not usually the case. Take care of
the emotional issues first so you can pursue your dreams with energy, commitment, and perseverance.

How to determine whether it's a personal problem or plain old fear

If you are immobilized, how can you know whether what's stopping
you is a personal problem or just plain old fear? Brenda's story
illustrates the difference.

Brenda's fear

When I met Brenda, she was in her early forties and had been
a successful public relations executive for ten years. She had
quit her job and was feeling dissatisfied, wanting to explore
"more meaningful" work.

Because she had earned and saved a lot of money, Brenda first took some time off. She traveled to foreign countries, visited friends in other states, took a foreign language class, attended many personal growth and healing workshops, read voraciously (usually self-help books), and took care of a sister during an illness. When we met, she had been unemployed for almost a year and was beginning to panic about money. She felt frustrated because she still did not know what she wanted to do, although she was enthusiastic when she talked about the healing professions.

During the career workshop, she made a commitment to work with people using body movement and artistic expression. She didn't yet have a title for the job or a clear picture of what it would look like, but she knew she eventually wanted to have a private practice of her own and move to California. It looked as if Brenda was launched. All she had to do was fill in the picture.

But two weeks later, she was back in my office, sounding as unsure about the future as she had the first day I met her. The next step she needed to take was to enroll in several training programs, one of which was six months long. She was scared to make the commitment. "What if it's wrong?" she kept asking. "I've already spent so much money. I've already taken so long. What if it's the wrong direction for me?"

At this point, Brenda certainly did not look like a person who had managed a high-powered career for ten years, nor did she feel like one. Her chosen profession was new, uncharted territory. It was also radically different from public relations work, and even though Brenda thought she had natural gifts for healing work, there was no guarantee that she would be successful and make a living at it.

Brenda was experiencing the normal fear of taking on the unknown, the fear that comes with moving toward a dream. When she talked about the training courses she needed to take, she became animated and enthusiastic. Brenda was healthy emotionally and physically, so she responded well to listening and encouragement from me and her friends and decided as a first step to enroll in a weeklong course in movement therapy. She loved it and decided to complete several more weeks of training in order to become certified. Then, with more support from me, she took the second step and enrolled in a six-month course in massage therapy to gain the foundation she would need for the rest of her work.

Brenda telephoned me after she completed the massage training. She said the training had been well worth the time and money. She had returned home only long enough to pack up her things and move; she had fallen in love with a man she'd met in the program and was moving to California to be with him. In addition, she had already begun working with several clients. Her new career was launched, and she was thrilled with the decisions she had made for herself. ●

Brenda listened to her heart and was able to move beyond her fears. New directions scare most of us. Even though we have had success in the past, when we embark on something totally new, we feel on some level that we are starting all over again. Internally, it is as if we are adolescents again. And the closer the dream is to our hearts, the more vulnerable and scared we feel.

That's all a normal part of the process. Simply being frightened and temporarily unable to take action is not a problem that requires therapy. All that's needed is support. However, if you are immobilized regardless of how much support others offer you and cannot get going no matter how hard you try, it may be time to acknowledge that you are not ready yet or that something else may be going on. Look honestly into your life—remember, reveal what's true for you. Do you have any of the six problems described in this chapter? If so, it may be time to seek help from a professional.

key 1	Reveal what's true for you
key 2	Reclaim your personal power
key 3	Express your commitment
key 4	Surround yourself with support

Questions to ask yourself

- If I am having trouble getting going with my career plans, what is really holding me back? Is it something I haven't acknowledged yet? Am I not feeling well physically? Are my relationships emotionally draining? Am I always pessimistic about the future? Do I seriously doubt that I can do what I want to? Am I worried that I may be depending too much on a drug? Do events from the past bother me and feel unresolved?

- If I have not been able to do anything by myself about moving my work and life along, why do I think I will be able to in the future? What will be different?

- What's keeping me from getting help? (Money cannot be an answer here because there are low-cost programs available through churches, social service agencies, and state and federal programs.)

Action steps to take

- If you have determined that a personal problem is holding you back or if you suspect this may be the case, read some self-help books addressing the problem. Listen to tapes. Attend seminars or meetings of self-help groups. Begin somewhere.

- Ask your priest, minister, rabbi, or spiritual advisor for advice.

- Ask for help from the employee assistance program in your company.

- Interview someone who openly admits being a recovered alcoholic, drug addict, or victim of abuse. Ask how the person did it and whether he or she has a counselor or program to recommend. Ask the person to go to a meeting with you if you need company.

Staying on course in your life is like tacking (changing direction when sailing)—you need to keep returning to your center, your core.

—a wise client

chapter 13
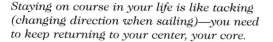avoid getting derailed

When you're questioning your future direction, everyone becomes an expert on what you should do. People deliver glib advice as if it's the obvious truth rather than just their personal opinion. Unfortunately, much of this advice is erroneous, based on ancient history, and worst of all, not even about you. Family and friends can be the worst.

I've often met with clients who were enthusiastic and confident about their future dreams one week and deeply discouraged the next, convinced they had made a wrong decision. When I ask, "What happened since we met?" they'll say, "Nothing." Skeptically, I'll ask, "Well, whom did you talk to about your dreams?"

"Nobody. Well, I did talk to my older sister" (substitute mother, boyfriend, best friend, dad).

"And how did that go?"

"Well, she thinks it will be too hard and I should do something else instead."

We don't become discouraged for no reason. There's always something that triggers it. Usually, it's a negative conversation with someone whose opinion we value and whose approval is important to us.

Be careful whom you reveal your dreams to, especially in the beginning stages. Don't confer the status of pope on people who are not experts or who are usually cynical and negative about work. And don't tell family members if you aren't ready to enroll them in your dreams. Wait until you feel stronger or have made some progress.

Bad advice to watch out for

The following are five examples of bad advice that are very common and can be derailing. Take all this advice from "experts" with more than a grain of salt and don't let it stand in your way. Trust your own intuition.

chart 10
five examples of bad advice to watch out for

1. "To find a good job, choose a good industry."
2. "Send out lots of résumés."
3. "Don't leave a job until you have another one."
4. "Never refuse a promotion."
5. "If you can't find what you want, just take a job and then keep looking."

"To find a good job, choose a good industry"

In despair, a friend once told me that her relatives were advising her younger brother, who was undertaking his first job search, to choose an industry in which lots of jobs were available. On the surface, this sounds like sensible advice, but it completely disregards what he might want to do or what might interest him. It's true that some industries may not have a lot of jobs, but then he didn't need a lot of jobs, just one.

If you are really interested in a certain industry or field, don't let the fact that it is crowded stop you. Every field contains a variety of related jobs. It is important, even when seeking your first job, to explore what you are interested in learning, doing, or becoming and then to find what looks like a good fit for you.

The importance of finding a good fit applies to people at every level, even those with doctoral degrees. Often, people who have earned advanced degrees in unusual subjects give up on finding work related to their degree. Denise is one person who didn't give up and found a creative way to use an obscure degree.

An obscure Ph.D. degree

Denise came to me for advice a few months after she had completed years of work on a Ph.D. degree in theology with a focus on the Bible. She was proud of the fact that she had earned a very difficult degree, and she was passionately interested in teaching. However, she was keenly aware that the market for teachers in her area of study was extremely limited. Teaching had always been her goal, and now she was confronted with the likelihood of not being able to get a job.

Denise was fifty-five years old, vital, and enthusiastic about working. "What else can I do?" she asked. "Where should I look for a job?" Denise's whole perspective changed in a matter of minutes when I suggested that she forget job hunting and instead think of herself as a generator of interesting projects. She was thrilled with this idea and immediately began thinking of places where she could teach one or two courses, including some in Europe; workshops and seminars she could lead; and papers she could write.

A week later, Denise called to tell me she had not been selected for the one teaching position she had the best chance at. She was disappointed but not discouraged because she now had lots of great ideas for other projects and different ways to teach. For example, she had shifted her focus from teaching seminary students to teaching experienced ministers, an area in which she saw an unmet need. Every minister with whom she had talked about the idea had been enthusiastic and encouraging. She had already scheduled a retreat for ministers to take place the following year. She had at least ten ideas for places to teach, including retirement centers where laypeople might be interested in learning more about the Bible. Denise felt excited and energized. She was going to make use of her many years of study and follow through with her commitment after all, although not in a traditional way. ●

Denise did not let a narrow market with few opportunities stop her from doing what she had a passion for. She just opened up her thinking. Advice to choose work based only on its availability is a form of "poverty consciousness." It overlooks the abundance in this world and disregards the ingenuity, creativity, and determination of impassioned human beings to create work they love doing.

"Send out lots of résumés"

I can't believe people are still giving this advice today. But commonly, people who have never done a job search or who haven't looked for work in twenty years tell their family members and friends to send out lots of résumés. Despite all the studies showing that this is one of the least effective ways to find a dream job, people still rely on this advice. Perhaps more important, it is also one of the least satisfying ways to look for work. Sending résumés to strangers is like sending mail into a black hole. There is no exchange of energy. Usually, the only response is an occasional computer-generated rejection letter.

This job search method reinforces passivity. It is a way to hide. You sit and wait until you hear from someone—not good. *Networking is the number one best way to land a job, period.* You should spend the majority of your time on this activity. Not only is it energizing to talk to people, but also jobs are sometimes created on the spot. Regardless, the contacts you make during your networking effort can pay off long after you land your job. They are potential resources for solving future problems, for embarking on joint ventures and partnerships, and for finding help if you have to look for work again.

Of course, there are exceptions. Some people land good jobs by sending out résumés and responding to newspaper advertisements. Do put some energy into these approaches, but have them make up only about 10 to 15 percent of your job search. The rest of your effort and time should go into networking.

"Don't leave a job until you have another one"

Due to merger and downsizing frenzy, periods of unemployment are common today. But many people, even career experts, still give this advice. I disagree. If you need to leave, you need to leave, whether you have another job or not.

How can you look for another job if it drains your energy just to go to work every day, if you are experiencing stress-related symptoms such as headaches or stomachaches, or if your current job is so demanding that you have no time to think about what you want to do with your life, much less look for something? In all these cases, it is much better to leave, creating some space to take on the next chapter in your life.

Today, unemployment does not carry the stigma that it once did. When interviewing for a job after a period of unemployment, just present your time off in an empowering way. For example, tell a prospective employer that you are rested and have taken the time to be sure that this is what you want to do. This will put you way ahead of a candidate who is exhausted and desperate to leave his or her current job.

"Never refuse a promotion"

This advice is based on the common "wisdom" that you'll ruin your chances for future promotions if you refuse one. Generally, I haven't seen that to be true with my clients. It's usually the opposite. Good people are often offered several opportunities for promotion, not just one. But regardless of whether the advice is true in your situation, it's based on the assumption that moving up the ladder is the most important thing in your life and the best thing for you to do. It ignores other aspects of your life that might be equally important or even more important to you. For example, if you are promoted, will you have to move? How do your spouse and children feel about it? Does the new position involve work you love, or will it take you farther away from your talents and passion? It's perfectly all right to make decisions based on these criteria, not just on how far you will advance within the company. Paying attention to these factors is a way to maintain integrity, authenticity, and happiness in your work and life.

Norm says no

Norm was an assistant manager of a large warehouse when I met him. He was in his late thirties, ambitious, eager to learn, and working on an M.B.A. degree. He was respected in his company and had recently been offered a job in a different department. When he turned it down, some of his colleagues told him he had missed a good opportunity and suggested that he might be averse to taking risks.

Norm told me that he wasn't afraid of taking a risk; he just had not been interested in the assignment he had been offered, and no one had supported him in his decision. We worked on clarifying what he wanted to do and what he had to offer. We agreed that the job had not been a good match with his interests and talents. Norm decided that he really liked warehousing, that it was a good fit, and that he wanted to stay in that area. He also saw that he was ready to step into a full leadership role and run a warehousing center himself.

Out of the blue, the company was sold to a much larger company and Norm's boss was promoted. The job of running the warehouse was open. Norm jumped at the chance, proving that he was definitely willing to take a risk in an area he loved. He got the job, and because of the size of the new company, there are possibilities for additional growth in the future. ●

"If you can't find what you want, just take a job and then keep looking"

This advice presumes that you have little or no integrity. It suggests that you would see nothing wrong with asking people to take a chance on you, give you whatever training you need, invest in you, and then lose you as soon as something better comes along.

This advice also doesn't take into account the fact that it's never easy to hold down a full-time job and conduct a job search at the same time. It's even harder when you are just starting a new job. Yes, it's exciting, but it's also exhausting. Nothing is familiar. It takes a while just to find your way around, much less master the job and cultivate new relationships. Your energy and attention are taken up with these concerns, leaving very little available for a job search. Finally, extricating yourself will probably be much more difficult than you think, especially if you tend to be loyal.

chart 11
seven dangerous assumptions to avoid

1. "If the going is tough, I'm not moving in the right direction."
2. "If I can't see a way to carry out my plans, they won't work."
3. "If the results don't match my expectations, I'm on the wrong track."
4. "It's too late."
5. "When I've saved enough money, I'll be able to do what I want."
6. "It will be better when I get to the top."
7. "I can have it all."

Seven dangerous assumptions to avoid

Bad advice is not the only thing to watch out for. We can just as easily get derailed by our own erroneous assumptions and myths. The following are seven common ones.

"If the going is tough, I'm not moving in the right direction"

The fact that a course of action is difficult doesn't mean it's wrong. If you're not accomplishing things as quickly or as easily as you had hoped you would, you might assume you are not doing it right or you made a wrong choice. My experience is that almost everything takes longer than I think it will and is harder than I imagine it will be (thank goodness we can't imagine it, or we might not do it). Creating a fulfilling work situation and a satisfying life takes time and determination. Remember: it's a process, not an event. It's important to keep your dreams and goals in front of you, to focus on what you really want and what's right for you, and to continue on the path regardless of how things look at any given moment.

Directing

When Beth came to me for advice, she had been in the theater world for ten years. Her goal was to become a full-time director. It had been a year since the last time we had sat down and talked.

Beth was discouraged and believed she was still far from her goal. But I heard the opposite. As she recounted all the plays she had directed during the last year, I recognized the momentum she was building. Although her directing work was still far from full-time, it was three times as much as she had done the year before.

Still, Beth thought maybe she should give up because pursuing her goal was so hard and was taking such a long time. She had been working on it on and off for four years. She asked, "How can you tell whether you're on the brink of a breakthrough or you should just quit?"

I told Beth that it didn't sound to me as if she were finished with theater yet. She wasn't cynical or sick of it, complaining about actors or the industry, or worn out. In fact, she had recently begun an intensive study of the work of a particular playwright, and in order to keep her skills up to date, she was enthusiastically attending every new play in town. I thought Beth's problem was that she was focusing only on the gap between where she was and where she wanted to be. She was not seeing the progress she had made.

Before she left, we set some new goals that were exciting to her and opened up more possibilities in other states. Beth was reenergized and ready to go again. ●

"If I can't see a way to carry out my plans, they won't work"

You don't need to know how you're going to do something before you start. You'll learn along the way, and you can always get help from people who do know. Think about the most gratifying accomplishments you've had in your life. Didn't they involve a good measure of not knowing in the beginning?

"If the results don't match my expectations, I'm on the wrong track"

Don't assume that a direction is wrong if everything doesn't turn out exactly as you envisioned it would. It probably won't. Life is full of twists, turns, and surprises, some good, some bad. But I have discovered that holding on to a picture of how something *should* be is limiting. Sometimes things turn out even better than we ever imagined them. Remember that dreams can become reality in many different ways.

"It's too late"

People often take detours from their goals, for any number of good reasons. Sometimes urgent family obligations prevent them from doing what they want at the time. Sometimes they are scared and not ready. Sometimes the time is just not right or they are sidetracked by an adventure or money. That's okay. If this describes you, it doesn't mean it's too late to start again. True, you may not be able to become a ballerina or a firefighter at the age of forty-five, but you *can* do work directly related to your love of dance or your wish to keep people safe from harm. In fact, you may discover that your past experiences inform your new work and contribute to your success.

"When I've saved enough money, I'll be able to do what I want"

People tell themselves that they will take the next large sum of money they get and pay off all their bills, and then they will be able to do what they want. This rarely happens. Instead, life keeps presenting us with unexpected expenses, and financial independence gets pushed further into the future.

A better strategy is to begin doing what you want to do right now, even in the smallest way, and keep building on that for the future. None of us is guaranteed a particular life expectancy. Why put off what you want to do? Stop postponing living your life fully. Live it now.

"It will be better when I get to the top"

The top may be better for some people, but for many it isn't. It's just better pay. If you aren't doing work you're passionate about and living a life you love, being at the top won't make any difference; you will feel just as empty and dissatisfied as before. In fact, some of my most successful clients have wondered why they put all their energy into getting there. And today, there are no guarantees that the top will even be there when you are ready for it. Companies come and companies go.

"I can have it all"

It's a trap to believe you can have it all. More likely, you can have much of it, not all at once but over the span of your life. Even then, there will be trade-offs. And that's not bad. It forces you to become clear about your priorities.

The danger is that you will think there's something wrong with *you* because you don't have it all or that you will push yourself even harder and miss the joy of what you do have right now. It's better to be kind to yourself, to avoid comparing yourself with others who have more, and to be grateful for what you have when you have it.

chart 12
four empowering thoughts to keep in mind

1. Work is only a human creation.
2. You are in charge of your own career.
3. Even if most people are unhappy at work, you don't have to be.
4. It's okay to say no.

Four empowering thoughts to keep in mind

Staying on course takes some work. You need to avoid derailment by bad advice, erroneous assumptions, and myths, and you must stay true to yourself. You will need some empowering thoughts to help you along the way. Here are four to keep in mind.

Work is only a human creation

Our ways of working are not carved in stone. We have forgotten that human beings made up work in the first place. Someone decided that a person who writes letters and answers the telephone should be called a secretary. Someone decided that the person who heads a company should be called a CEO and other workers should be arranged in a hierarchy.

As a human being, you can make up work any way you want it to be, especially if you are self-employed. Even if you aren't, you still have the power to voice your opinion, create projects, and even start new enterprises within your company. The key is to respond to needs. Look to see what's wanted, needed, or missing, and then create work to fill those gaps. That's all human beings have ever done.

You are in charge of your own career

Your mother isn't in charge of your career. Your father isn't. Even your boss isn't. Only you can know what you really want to be doing and what your full range of gifts is. Regardless of what other people think and want for you, it is up to you to follow your own path.

Even if most people are unhappy at work, you don't have to be

Since you are in charge of your own career, it's up to you to find work that interests you, work that leaves you feeling proud of yourself and satisfied. Find people who love what they are doing, and spend time with them. They're out there. It's inspiring to be around them. If you don't know anybody who loves his or her work, you're hanging around with the wrong people.

It's okay to say no

It's okay to say no to job offers that aren't right for you; promotions that would take you away from what you are passionate about and good at; behavior that you believe is unethical or immoral; or more work than any one person can do and still have a life outside of work. Saying no is one way to get closer to what is right for you. Just have the courage to do it.

To stay on course, you may have to pull yourself back again and again to your center, to the place where who you are resides: your passions, yearnings, visions, talents, and values. Each time you get back on track, you will be stronger. You will feel renewed by finding yourself again. Your heart is always your best guide back to your center. Listen to it and trust what you know to be true.

key 1	Reveal what's true for you
key 2	Reclaim your personal power
key 3	Express your commitment
key 4	Surround yourself with support

Questions to ask yourself

- If I am contemplating a career move, is it the right next step for me? Is it really on my chosen path? Is it a detour (another way to get there), or is it a sidetrack?

- Am I looking to others rather than to myself for future direction?

- Am I telling people what I want, or am I just thinking about it a lot? Am I creating situations in which I communicate face-to-face with people about what I want instead of hiding behind paper (résumés, memos, letters)?

Action steps to take

- As often as possible—at least once a week—talk to the people in your life who support your goals and understand your desires. (Don't seek out people who you know will discourage or derail your efforts.)

- Look at a map. Choose a destination. Notice all the different ways to get there, including the twisting, winding roads.

- Meet with a friend who knows your dreams and is willing to be ruthlessly honest with you. Ask this person whether he or she thinks the next step you are considering is the right one for you.

I can't tell whether I'm in a rut or a groove.

—a client who always makes me laugh

chapter 14

going full circle

Congratulations! You used the four keys to finding fulfillment at work to design a work situation that was satisfying and a life you loved. You took steps that transformed your work right where you were, moved on to a new company where the fit was perfect, started a business of your own that you loved, or began an exciting new career. Whatever you did, it was perfect for you and you were thrilled, sure that this would be *it* for the rest of your life.

Everything went really well, perhaps for years. But then, one day, a familiar feeling of lethargy and uneasiness resurfaced. You found yourself beginning to dread Mondays again. How could this be? You had been doing such great work for so long. But life changes. We change. What was right once may not be right now.

But I thought this was going to be it!

We look at things differently as we grow older. Our values become more important to us. We resurrect some of the values we grew up with and create new ones based on wisdom and life experience. We are shaped by events, some tragic, some wonderful. Our priorities change. We come to terms with our shortcomings. Our energy is different; sometimes we have less of it for the things we used to do. We become ever more acutely aware of the temporary nature of life and the fact that time is running out. We have much less tolerance for things we consider unimportant or artificial. What is important to us in our thirties is not important later on. And sometimes, once we have "arrived," our destination isn't what we thought it would be; we're disappointed. Or perhaps the company we work for is bought and sold and bought again, or grows wildly, or disappears entirely. Some of us benefit from the changes; others of us are hurt by them. If we're still with the company, we may become aware that it isn't the same place we signed on with. We admit that it's no longer a good fit. So, just when we thought we had our work situation pretty well settled, we may need to make dramatic changes again. This can happen more than once and when we least expect it. It's no wonder that we often feel in turmoil about our work and lives.

If any of this is happening to you, turn again to Chapter 1 and review the four keys to finding fulfillment at work. Ask yourself whether it's the work or the workplace that's the problem. Would changing the way you're working make the difference? Small but dramatic changes might be reenergizing. If not, is it time to leave your current work environment and do something totally different, perhaps even "retire" to a new life?

Even career experts who love their work are not immune to the turmoil that can hit. After fourteen years of leading career workshops—work that I passionately loved—I became restless and began questioning whether this was the work I really wanted to do. The feeling was familiar. It had led me to create this career for myself in the first place, and yet here I was again. I found the situation embarrassing. After all, as a career consultant, I was supposed to know what I wanted to do.

I turned again to the four keys and used them. As part of the process, I even met with a career coach a couple of times because I had decided that "the cobbler needed shoes." Through this process of reflection, I rediscovered my passion for my work. Ultimately, I concluded that I was still in the right field but needed to do two things: (1) restructure my business and (2) open up a new means of expression in my work. Writing became the new means of expression. To my surprise, I discovered that I'm as passionate about writing as I was about leading workshops. This book is an outgrowth of that time.

I was lucky. I was able to continue on my chosen career path just by redesigning the way I worked. One of my clients, Julia, did the same thing. After thirty-two years of working as a nurse, administrator, and teacher, she started a business as a health care consultant. She now guides and assists others in reaching their goals in the health care industry. She reported in a letter that this career change has given her the "opportunity to see the personal power and dignity that was within me so I could release it to support others" and "is the best thing I ever did for myself."

Stan is another person who continued his work but in a new way and in a new setting.

Trading

When I met Stan, he was forty-six years old, the father of three children, and miserable in his work. He was a trader who was "burned out" after twenty years on the trading floor. Stan thought that to be happy again, he would probably have to change his career entirely, and we began exploring his interests. In the meantime, in order to feel better immediately, he left the trading floor and began working from his home, conducting his transactions over the Internet. He was surprised to discover that he really liked working this way. He was glad to be away from what he described as the craziness of the trading floor and felt much calmer. He was able to concentrate on his work and was making better trades.

He was surprised to discover that he also loved the lifestyle. He had time to exercise, take the dog for long walks, meet people in the neighborhood, and spend time with his kids. He also found time for volunteer work. Stan was so much happier in his new life that he decided to remain a trader as long as it continued to work well for him. ●

Paul also made dramatic changes in his work, as the following story illustrates.

Back to a first love

Paul was in his late fifties when I met him and had worked in advertising all his life. Most of those years had been happy, but now he found himself hating his work. The field had changed; it was more complex. The company had changed; it had grown and was no longer an intimate, familylike place. And as he had moved up in the company, his managing job had taken him further and further away from the projects he loved. Now all he did all day was fight fires. Paul said it wasn't fun anymore. In fact, it was very stressful.

Paul also had Crohn's disease, and recent flare-ups had warned him that this was not a healthy lifestyle for him. After examining what he wanted to do, Paul surprised all his colleagues by quitting his job. He decided to take some time off and then begin working from home, doing a variety of different things: freelance advertising projects he really liked, teaching, and some volunteering. When I spoke with Paul several months later, he reported that his pace was much more manageable, he was doing what he loved, and he was energized, happy, and healthy. ●

Carla, on the other hand, changed primarily how much she worked. She was a marketing expert who was highly valued by her company. However, when the company was bought out, a new management regime came in, and soon the handwriting was on the wall. Carla knew her job would be eliminated and she would have to leave, but she wasn't sad. It was the perfect time to fulfill her dream of working three days a week, at a job much closer to home, and writing her novel on the other two days.

Changing the way you work and staying in the same field isn't always possible; nor is it always the best answer. Sometimes you have to put an end to what you are doing and design something entirely new. You have to reinvent yourself and find a new sense of purpose.

On to great mondays again

Whatever the case may be for you, use the four keys again to find fulfillment at work. Begin with key #1 and reveal what's true for you *now*. Trust the wisdom of your heart as you answer these questions: What's true for me *now*, at this stage of my life? What am I yearning to do *now*? If I could have it any way I wanted it *now*, what would it look like?

Then use key #2 to reclaim your personal power. Remind yourself that you are not a victim. You are not condemned to an unhappy work situation for the rest of your life. Take ownership of what you have created so far, all the good and the bad. Remember that you are in charge of your life. You can redesign it the way you want it to be. Then get into action. Do something. Just get started.

Move on to key #3 and express your commitment. After you have conducted an internal search (and maybe an external one, too), make a choice about a new future. Then coordinate your actions with your commitment. Keep going; don't give up.

Make sure to use key #4 and surround yourself with support. Gather people around you who believe in you, people who will challenge you to be your best and to follow through on your dreams and visions.

You will probably need to use the four keys many times in order to experience satisfying, fulfilling, and empowering work throughout your lifetime. That's okay. It doesn't mean anything's wrong. It's just an acknowledgment of the dynamic nature of life and the need for all of us to continue growing emotionally, intellectually, and spiritually. Use the keys every time you undergo a major transition. If you do, I promise you'll be looking forward not only to weekends but also to Mondays.

key 1	Reveal what's true for you
key 2	Reclaim your personal power
key 3	Express your commitment
key 4	Surround yourself with support

Questions to ask yourself

- Is it time to redesign my life?

- Do I need to take a sabbatical and rest for a while before making any major decisions?

- What have I always wanted to do in my work and haven't done yet? How could I do it now?

Action steps to take

- Find people who have redesigned their lives in their later years and are happy with the results. Ask them how they did it.

- Pray and ask the Creator for guidance.

- Review Part One of this book and carry out the process all over again. It works!

the author

With over thirty years of experience as a counselor, consultant, trainer, and teacher, Robin Sheerer is an expert in coaching people on career-life issues. Since founding Career Enterprises Incorporated in 1981, she has designed and led workshops on career issues, personal effectiveness, leadership, and team building; facilitated support groups of entrepreneurs and people engaged in career transition; coached thousands of people in career-life planning; and provided consultation to numerous companies. Her clients have included Allstate, DDB Needham Worldwide, Federal

Reserve Bank, John Nuveen & Co., Inc., Recycled Paper Products, Sibson & Company, and Swiss Air, among many others.

Prior to starting her own business, Sheerer worked in the social services, taught at the City Colleges of Chicago and the University of Illinois, and had a part-time private practice in psychotherapy. She holds a B.A. degree in sociology/anthropology from Antioch College, an M.A. degree from the School of Social Service Administration, University of Chicago, and a certificate from National Training Laboratories in Human Resource Utilization with a special focus on Affirmative Action Applications. The recipient of an award for excellence in training and consulting from the Chicago chapter of the American Society for Training and Development, Sheerer is a dynamic speaker and is frequently sought as a presenter and keynote speaker.

Sheerer lives in Oak Park, Illinois, with her husband, Earl Lemberger, and a feisty schnauzer named Molly. Her hobbies include reading mysteries and novels, camping, and knitting afghans with a Warm up America! group.

resources

For Help with Career and Work Choices

Anderson, N. *Work with Passion* (New World Library, 1995).

Beyer, C., Pike, D., and McGovern, L. *Surviving Unemployment: A Family Handbook for Weathering Hard Times* (Henry Holt, 1993).

Bolles, R. N. *The Quick Job Hunting Map* (a shorter version of *What Color Is Your Parachute?*; Ten Speed Press).

Bolles, R. N. *What Color Is Your Parachute?* (published annually; Ten Speed Press).

Edwards, P., and Edwards, S. *Finding Your Perfect Work: The New Career Guide to Making a Living, Creating a Life* (Tarcher/Putnam, 1996).

Hudson, F. *The Adult Years: Mastering the Art of Self-Renewal* (Jossey-Bass, 1991).

Hudson, F., and McLean, P. *Life Launch: A Passionate Guide to the Rest of Your Life* (Hudson Institute Press. 1995).

Lloyd, C. *Creating a Life Worth Living: A Practical Course in Career Design for Artists, Innovators, and Others Aspiring to a Creative Life* (Harper-Perennial, 1997).

Sher, B., and Gottlieb, A. *Wishcraft* (Ballantine, 1986).

Sher, B., with Smith, B. *I Could Do Anything If I Only Knew What It Was* (Delacorte, 1994).

Sinetar, M. *Do What You Love, The Money Will Follow: Discovering Your Right Livelihood* (Paulist Press, 1987).

Winter, B. *Making a Living Without Having a Job: Winning Ways for Creating Work That You Love* (Bantam, 1993).

On Work

Bridges, W. *Job Shift: How to Prosper in a Workplace Without Jobs* (Addison-Wesley, 1994).

Bridges, W. *Transitions: Strategies for Coping with the Difficult, Painful, and Confusing Times in Your Life* (Addison-Wesley, 1980).

Covey, S. *The 7 Habits of Highly Effective People* (Simon & Schuster, 1989).

Fox, M. *The REinvention of Work: A New Vision of Livelihood for Our Time* (HarperSanFrancisco, 1994).

Frankel, L. *JUMP-START Your Career: 8 Reasons Why Successful People Derail and How to Get Back on Track* (Three Rivers Press, 1998).

Goleman, D. *Emotional Intelligence: Why It Can Matter More Than IQ* (Bantam, 1997).

Hawken, P. *Growing a Business* (Simon & Schuster, 1987).

Hawken, P. *The Next Economy* (Ballantine, 1983).

Kelley, R. *How to Be a Star at Work: Nine Breakthrough Strategies You Need to Succeed* (Times Business Random House, 1998).

McKenna, E. P. *When Work Doesn't Work Any More: Women, Work, and Identity* (Delacorte, 1997).

Popcorn, F. *The Popcorn Report: Faith Popcorn on the Future of Your Company, Your World, Your Life* (HarperBusiness, 1991).

Tannen, D. *You Just Don't Understand: Women and Men in Conversation* (Ballantine Books, 1990).

Wright, H. *How to Make a Thousand Mistakes in Business and Still Succeed* (The Wright Track, 1990).

On Creativity

Cameron, J. *The Artist's Way: A Spiritual Path to Higher Creativity* (Tarcher/Perigee, 1992).

Fritz, R. *The Path of Least Resistance: Learning to Become the Creative Force in Your Own Life* (Fawcett Columbine, 1989).

Gawain, S. *Creative Visualization* (Bantam, 1983).

For Inspiration

Breathnach, S. B. *Simple Abundance: A Daybook of Comfort and Joy* (Warner Books, 1995).

Chopra, D. *The Seven Spiritual Laws of Success: A Practical Guide to the Fulfillment of Your Dreams* (Amber-Allen Publishing and New World Library, 1993).

Hyatt, C., and Gottlieb, L. *When Smart People Fail: Rebuilding Yourself for Success* (Penguin Books, 1993).

Jeffers, S. *Feel the Fear and Do It Anyway* (Fawcett Columbine, 1987).

For Career-Related Negotiation Skills

Chapman, J. *Negotiating Your Salary: How to Make $1000 a Minute* (Ten Speed Press, 1996)

Other Related Topics

Dlugozima, H., Scott, J., and Sharp, D. *Six Months Off: How to Plan, Negotiate, and Take the Break You Need Without Burning Bridges or Going Broke* (Henry Holt, 1996).

Dominguez, J., and Robin, V. *Your Money or Your Life: Transforming Your Relationship with Money and Achieving Financial Independence* (Penguin Books, 1992).

Keeffe, C. *How to Get What You Want in Life with the Money You Already Have: Simple Yet Revolutionary Ideas for Reaching Your Dreams While Still Paying the Bills* (Little, Brown, 1995).

Orman, S. *The 9 Steps to Financial Freedom* (Crown, 1997).

St. James, E. *Living the Simple Life* (Hyperion, 1996).

index

Career Enterprises Resources

_____ **KEYNOTE PRESENTATIONS, SEMINARS, & WORKSHOPS**
For information, fill out and mail in the form below, or call
708-524-4850.

_____ **AUDIOTAPE** $10.00
Empower Your Career: 4 Keys to Success
An inspiring and motivating tape to listen to over and over
again. Perfect for your car. Format includes questions to
reflect on and apply to your life.

_____ **MANUAL** $69.95
_The ART of Career Coaching: Empowering People
to Live Their Dreams_
A guide on how to work successfully with clients or employees.
Learn how to help people identify their goals and move through
resistance and obstacles to achieve them. Advice on how to set
up a business of your own as a career coach. For beginners or
experienced practitioners.

_____ **PACKAGE** (8% discount) $73.56
Audiotape and manual

Call for information on quantity discounts.

Subtotal _____

Shipping: $2.00 per tape; $4.00 per manual; $5.00 per package _____

IL residents add 8.75% sales tax _____

TOTAL _____

(over)

TO ORDER

Send check to:

Career Enterprises Incorporated
300 North Maple #3
Oak Park, IL 60302
Fax: 708-524-4836
Tel: 708-524-4850
Toll free: 888-344-4554
E-mail: careerprz@aol.com

Or order via credit card:
❏ VISA   ❏ MasterCard

Name on card _____

Account number _____

Signature _____ Expiration date _____

SHIP TO

Name _____

Address _____

City_____ State _____ Zip _____

Company _____

Title _____

Day Telephone (   ) _____